GOD,
IN EVERY STEP

AUTHOR
BERMIE DIZON

GOD,

IN EVERY STEP

AUTHOR

BERMIE DIZON

Acknowledgments

This book was made possible through the support, encouragement, and love of so many. First and foremost, I am grateful to God, who has walked with me in every step, moment, and season and has been present in every lesson shared here.

To my family, my constant sources of joy, strength, and inspiration—thank you for your love and understanding throughout this journey. To my wife, Millet, whose wisdom and patience have blessed me beyond words. To my children, Ben, Carmel, Abel, and David, who remind me daily of God's grace and unfailing love.

My siblings—Henrietta, Ferdinand, Ahmed, Eriz (now passed), and Arnel—have been a tremendous source of encouragement to me. I am equally grateful to my parents, Bienvenido and Verlantina, who are also no longer with us; their lives have deeply inspired many of the devotionals in this book, and I carry such beautiful memories of them. My mother-in-law, Rosie, has also played a significant role in my life, embodying unconditional love and selfless service to her children.

I am deeply thankful for the community of believers who have walked alongside me, especially the members of my faith community, **Grace Communion International**, and friends from various denominations and congregations who have encouraged me over the years. Your prayers and friendship have strengthened my faith and inspired me to keep serving.

A special thanks to my friends in the Philippines who, after reading my Facebook online posts, responded with encouragement and suggested that I compile my weekly devotionals into a printed book and an e-book.

I am grateful to **GLOW (God Loves Our World) Missions International** for co-sponsoring this project. Their support has been instrumental in bringing this book to fruition.

Finally, to every reader of this book, thank you for inviting these reflections into your life. May this devotional encourage you, inspire you, and remind you that the God who loves you deeply is with you in every step of your life.

Table of Contents

Introduction

Welcome to *God, in Every Step*. In this devotional journey, I hope that each week you will be drawn closer to God as you reflect on His boundless love and unwavering faithfulness. Through the highs and lows of my own life, I have come to see God's hand guiding, comforting, and sustaining me in every step, and I am eager to share this journey with you.

Most of the devotionals in this book are inspired by my walk with God—times when I've felt His presence profoundly and times when I've had to trust Him in the unknown. In each step and each moment, God has always been there. He is truly our Comforter, our Encourager, and our Guide.

Life brings moments of joy, but it also brings challenges that can feel overwhelming. In every circumstance—whether in times of celebration or in the valleys of despair—God is with us. He walks beside us, providing grace and strength, reminding us that we are never alone. He is present in our successes and our struggles, in our ordinary days and our greatest trials.

In these pages, I invite you to reflect on personal experiences, challenges, and victories, while grounding yourself in the truth of Scripture. Each week, you will find a devotional designed to inspire and uplift, followed by reflection questions, a concluding thought, prayer prompts, and scriptures to meditate on. These elements are here to help you apply what you've read and discover God's hand at work in your own life.

As you journey through this book, I pray you will come to see that God is not distant. He is actively involved in every detail of your life. He knows your deepest needs, celebrates your joys, and shares in your sorrows. No matter where you are on your journey, remember that He is always near—present, mindful, and filled with love and grace for you. May you find peace, encouragement, and a renewed sense of God's presence as you walk with Him, step by step.

Week 1: A New Beginning

In 1995, my parents were 75 and 72 years old when they were forced to leave their beloved home. It was an unimaginable event—one of nature's raw and unpredictable forces. Heavy rains poured down, triggering the release of volcanic debris from the sides of Mt. Pinatubo. This debris, a torrent of thick mud, ash, and rocks, known as lahar, surged down the mountain, swallowing entire villages, including my parents' home.

The force of the lahar was overwhelming. It buried everything in its path, sparing only the roof of my parents' house. For two agonizing days, my parents were trapped in their home, without food or water, as the mud solidified around them, hard and cold. It was a miracle they survived.

At the time, I was living on another island, Mindanao. When I heard the news, I rushed to their aid. I knew they couldn't stay. The devastation was too great, and the threat too real. I urged them to move to a safer place, another province where we could start anew. My mother, though heartbroken, agreed. But my father, in his stubborn pride, refused. "I will die where I was born and raised," he declared.

Convincing him to leave wasn't easy. He was a man of the old ways, bound to his land and his memories. But finally, I looked him in the eye and said, "Dad, it's better to start a new life than to end one." Those words touched something deep within him. Reluctantly, he agreed to move. Sometimes, especially for the elderly, change feels like the hardest thing in the world. But often, it's necessary for survival, for growth, and for a new beginning. Thanks to my siblings who helped in building a new home for them.

Life is filled with moments where we feel overwhelmed—by problems, by mistakes, by the sheer weight of the past. But God's mercies are new every morning. His love greets us with the dawn, inviting us to let go of yesterday's burdens and step into a fresh start. This isn't just a comforting thought—it's the reality of His unwavering presence. No matter our age or circumstance, His Spirit is always ready to renew us.

The words of Lamentations 3:22-23 ring true: "Because of the Lord's great love we are not consumed, for His compassions never fail. They are new every morning; great is Your faithfulness."

Imagine the Holy Spirit as the ultimate reset button. Like a computer that reboots and restores itself to full function, the Spirit breathes new life into our weary souls. This isn't about forgetting the past; it's about allowing God to transform it. His faithfulness doesn't just wipe the slate clean—He empowers us to step forward with fresh strength.

How liberating it is to know we're never truly stuck. Our failures don't define us, and our past doesn't confine us. Each day is a new opportunity to lean into His compassion. No matter how many times we've stumbled or fallen, His love resets our hearts and gives us another chance.

The Bible is full of stories of people who found renewal in God. Moses spent forty years as a shepherd before God called him to lead a nation. Ruth, a Moabite widow, left everything she knew to follow her mother-in-law Naomi and found redemption in a foreign land, becoming part of the lineage of Jesus. David, despite his grave sin with Bathsheba, found forgiveness and a renewed relationship with God. These stories remind us that God doesn't give up on us, even in our darkest moments.

With God, you don't have to wait for the "perfect" moment to begin again. His mercies meet us every day, inviting us to walk forward in hope. Today can be that fresh start if we trust in His faithful love.

Concluding Thought:

Life is full of unexpected challenges and difficult transitions, just like my parents' journey from their home of many years to a new beginning. Change, especially when it is forced upon us, can feel overwhelming. Yet, through all the storms and trials, we can trust that God's mercies are new every morning. His faithfulness never wavers, and His Spirit empowers us to start again, no matter how daunting it may seem. With God, every day is an opportunity for renewal, and He walks with us through every transition, no matter how painful or difficult it might be.

Closing Prayer:

Heavenly Father, we thank You for Your unfailing love and compassion that are new every morning. When life's storms overwhelm us and we face hard transitions, remind us that You are always with us, offering hope and renewal. Help us to let go of our fears, our past, and even our pride, so that we may embrace the fresh start You give us. Grant us the courage to move forward in faith, knowing that Your plans are always for our good and that Your Spirit will always lead us to new life. In Jesus' name, Amen.

Reflection Questions:

1. Have you ever faced a situation where you had to make a difficult change in your life? How did you handle it, and what role did faith play in your decision?
2. What is one area of your life where you feel God is inviting you to start anew?

3. Why do you think change is so hard for many people, especially as we grow older? How can God help us through those transitions?
4. What burdens from the past are you holding onto that you need to release to experience God's fresh mercies each day?

Scriptures for Meditation:

- Lamentations 3:22-23 NIV: "Because of the Lord's great love we are not consumed, for His compassions never fail. They are new every morning; great is Your faithfulness."
- Isaiah 43:18-19 NIV: "Forget the former things; do not dwell on the past. See, I am doing a new thing! Now it springs up; do you not perceive it? I am making a way in the wilderness and streams in the wasteland."
- 2 Corinthians 5:17 NIV: "Therefore, if anyone is in Christ, the new creation has come: The old has gone, the new is here!"
- Philippians 1:6 NIV: "Being confident of this, that He who began a good work in you will carry it on to completion until the day of Christ Jesus."

Week 2: What We Think About God

"From A.W. Tozer's book *The Knowledge of the Holy*, this quote caught my attention: *"What comes into our minds when we think about God is the most important thing about us."*

What Tozer is suggesting is that the way we see God acts as a mirror, reflecting who we really are.

When we imagine God as loving and caring, it's as though we're saying, *"I believe in kindness and compassion."* On the flip side, if we see God as strict or punishing, it might reveal that we take some satisfaction in the suffering of others. Our concept of God is like a snapshot of our innermost thoughts and feelings.

When we see God loving us unconditionally and even sending His Son to die for our sake, how can we not be compelled to love Him back and extend that love to others?

How do you see God? This question is crucial because it influences who we are and how we behave. Consider this: When we pray or talk to God, it's not just about asking for things. Our prayers reveal what is important to us. If we pray for strength, it shows that we value resilience. If we ask for guidance, it tells a story about our desire for direction and purpose.

Here's the interesting part—sometimes our understanding of God also reveals our struggles. If we picture God as distant or indifferent, it could be a sign that we are feeling isolated or disconnected. Our concept of God becomes a roadmap, pointing to the state of our emotional and spiritual health.

So, take a moment to reflect on the God you believe in. What does that reveal about your own heart and soul?

As the Psalmist says in Psalm 139:23-24, *"Search me, O God, and know my heart; test me and know my anxious thoughts. See if there is any offensive way in me, and lead me in the way everlasting."* Let God's loving nature and infinite wisdom shape how we see Him and, ultimately, ourselves."

Concluding Thought:

The way we see God shapes not only our relationship with Him but also how we relate to others. If we view God as compassionate, loving, and present, it encourages us to embrace those same qualities in our lives. Let's strive to see God as He truly is—loving, caring, and deeply involved in every aspect of our lives.

Closing Prayer:

Heavenly Father, help us to see You as You truly are. Remove any distorted views we have of You and replace them with the truth of Your love, grace, and compassion. May our understanding of You shape our lives, leading us to love others as You have loved us. In Jesus' name, Amen.

Reflection Questions:

1. How do you currently see God, and how does that shape your relationship with Him and others?
2. In what ways can your understanding of God grow deeper and more aligned with His true nature?
3. How does your concept of God influence the way you handle challenges or difficulties in your life?

Scripture for Meditation:

- Psalm 103:8 – "The Lord is compassionate and gracious, slow to anger, abounding in love."
- 1 John 4:16 – "And so we know and rely on the love God has for us. God is love. Whoever lives in love lives in God, and God in them."

Week 3: In the Midst of Pain

We have all experienced pain or discrimination at some point in our lives, but there is one powerful story in the Bible where a woman endured both simultaneously. This took place during Jesus' ministry while He was walking with His disciples.

When she heard about Jesus, the woman came up behind Him in the crowd and touched His cloak, believing, *"If I just touch His clothes, I will be healed."* Immediately, her bleeding stopped, and she felt in her body that she had been freed from her suffering. At once, Jesus realized that power had gone out from Him. He turned around in the crowd and asked, *"Who touched My clothes?"*

The disciples, seeing the crowd pressing around Him, replied, *"You see the people crowding against You, and yet You can ask, 'Who touched Me?'"* But Jesus kept looking to see who had done it. Then the woman, knowing what had happened to her, came forward. Trembling with fear, she fell at His feet and told Him the whole truth. Jesus said to her, *"Daughter, your faith has healed you. Go in peace and be freed from your suffering"* (Mark 5:27-34, NIV).

Although the woman's name is not mentioned, her remarkable story of faith continues to inspire us never to give up. She had been living in the shadows, but she bravely stepped forward, determined to get closer to Jesus. Despite being considered an outcast due to her condition, she took the risk of approaching the Lord.

There are times when we find ourselves in a similar place. We may feel stuck in our pain, worrying that things will never change. Yet, like the woman, we can choose to press on in faith. Her story reminds us that there is always more to discover in our relationship with Jesus. We don't have to remain trapped in our struggles, blind to the new opportunities God is opening for us.

The world is full of bad news, and perhaps we are carrying bad news of our own. It can be overwhelming and confusing. Yet, God reveals Himself to us, walking with us through the crowds of our lives, helping us see Him amid our struggles. Remember, this woman had been suffering for 12 long years. She had visited many doctors, spent everything she had, and only grew worse. According to the customs of the time, she was considered unclean—sick, broke, and marginalized. But Jesus knew her situation, and He wanted us, as readers, to learn from her example.

It was her faith in Jesus that empowered her to overcome her pain, and when she reached out to Him, it changed everything.

Concluding Thought:

We often feel stuck in our struggles, believing that our pain and circumstances will never change. Yet, this story reminds us that faith and the courage to seek Jesus can lead to profound transformation. Even when obstacles seem to surround us, Jesus is there, ready to respond to our faith and bring healing to our lives. Let us take the risk of faith and trust that Jesus is near, moving through the crowds of our struggles.

Reflection Questions:

1. How does the story of the woman with the issue of blood inspire your faith in difficult times?
2. What risks do you need to take to draw closer to Jesus in your struggles?

Closing Prayer:

Dear Lord, thank You for being with me in the midst of my pain. Help me to have the courage and faith, like the woman in the crowd, to reach out to You in my times of need. Give me the strength to trust that You are near, even when I cannot see a way forward. I place my struggles in Your hands, knowing that You bring healing and peace. In Jesus' name, Amen.

Scripture for Meditation:

1. Psalm 34:18 (NIV) – "The Lord is close to the brokenhearted and saves those who are crushed in spirit."
2. Matthew 11:28 (NIV) – "Come to me, all you who are weary and burdened, and I will give you rest."

Week 4: Viewing the Milky Way

There are moments in life that pull us out of the ordinary and fill us with awe. One such moment happened recently when my son Abel invited me to Joshua Tree National Park in California to witness the Milky Way. A few days earlier, I had shared with him that I had never seen the Milky Way clearly, and in love, he made plans to show me the grandeur of the night sky.

The drive was two and a half hours long, but the timing couldn't have been better—there was a new moon, meaning the sky would be at its darkest, allowing the stars to shine in their full brilliance. A quick search confirmed that Joshua Tree is one of the best places to see the Milky Way during a new moon, particularly in the summertime. My wife joined us, along with my son David and his wife Holli. We packed folding chairs, a telescope, and binoculars, and set out for a night in the wilderness.

As we settled into our chairs and gazed upward, the sight that met our eyes left us speechless. The Milky Way stretched across the sky, a shimmering river of stars that declared the infinite creativity of God. Through the telescope, we marveled at Saturn and its majestic rings—a sight both distant and breathtakingly near.

Sitting there, surrounded by my family and the vastness of the cosmos, I couldn't help but reflect on the words of King David in Psalm 8:4: *"What is man that you are mindful of him?"* The sheer magnitude of creation was staggering. Here we were, on a small planet in a vast universe, yet God, the Creator of all, is mindful of us.

My sons, both engineers at JPL-NASA, filled the evening with fascinating facts about the universe—things I had never known before. Their knowledge only deepened my awe of the God who created the stars and allowed us to explore them. Holli and I were moved to talk about who we are as created beings and the true meaning of life.

As the hours passed and the night deepened, we reluctantly packed up and headed home, arriving around 2 a.m. But the late hour didn't matter. The experience was worth every minute. On the quiet drive back, I felt an overwhelming sense of God's presence. It was as though the night sky itself was a canvas painted with His love for humanity—a love that sustains not only us but the entire universe.

That evening reminded me of the vastness of God's creation and His intimate care for each of us. The same God who set the stars in place is the One who knows our deepest needs and loves us beyond measure. It was a night I will never forget—a night that left me in awe of the One who holds the cosmos in His hands and yet is mindful of you and me.

Colossians 1:17 says that Jesus is before all things, and in Him, all things hold together. The God who holds the universe together is the same God who holds your life together, even in the moments when you feel small or insignificant.

Concluding Thought:

As you go about your day, pause to take in the wonder of creation. Whether it's the sunrise, the stars at night, or the gentle breeze, remember that the Creator of all this beauty loves and cares for you personally. You are not forgotten. In the grand scheme of the universe, you are cherished by the One who holds everything together.

Closing Prayer:

Heavenly Father, thank You for the beauty of Your creation and for reminding us of Your majesty. Help us to see Your hand in the ordinary and extraordinary moments of our lives. May we always be in awe of Your love, knowing that You hold both the universe and our hearts in Your hands. In Jesus' name, Amen.

Reflection Questions:

1. Have you ever experienced a moment in nature that filled you with awe and wonder? How did it deepen your understanding of God?
2. When you consider the vastness of the universe, how does it make you feel about God's care for you?
3. What is one area of your life where you need to be reminded that God is holding things together?

Scripture for Meditation:

- Psalm 8:3-4 - "When I consider your heavens, the work of your fingers, the moon and the stars, which you have set in place, what is mankind that you are mindful of them, human beings that you care for them?"
- Colossians 1:17 - "He is before all things, and in Him all things hold together."

Week 5: Is Prayer Our Last Resort?

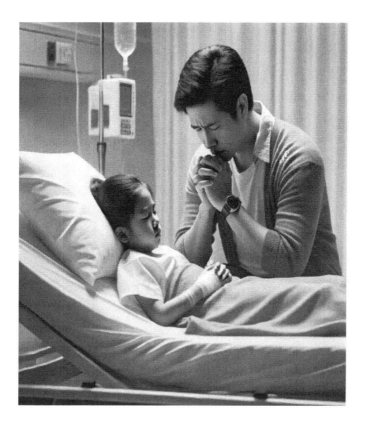

A few years ago, when my 88-year-old mother had a stroke, I called 911 for an ambulance to take her immediately to the hospital. After that, I contacted family members and asked for their prayers. Relatives who lived nearby came quickly to be with me and my family. We prayed together as we awaited further medical diagnoses. Church friends also came to visit my mom, and it was inspiring to witness them praying over her. I'm sure they noticed the worried look on my face, and their presence and prayers were a great comfort.

One thing I noticed during this experience was that when troubles come, we pray. I found this to be very good, as it brought me both comfort and encouragement.

However, this experience also made me reflect: Is prayer our last resort? Shouldn't prayer be our first line of defense? Often, it's when the doctor says, "There's nothing more we can do," that we turn to prayer. But prayer is not just our defense—it's our strongest offense against the powers that try to pull us down.

The Bible tells us, *"Do not be anxious about anything, but in every situation, by prayer and petition, with thanksgiving, present your requests to God"* (Philippians 4:6, NIV). Prayer is a conversation with God. It's speaking to Him with the assurance that He hears and cares. Prayer should be a way of life for Christians, something we do daily and regularly. Shouldn't we pray before doing anything at all?

Prayer should never be our last resort. In His Word, God encourages us to bring everything to Him in prayer. Wouldn't it be better if we prayed for each other when we're healthy and not just when we're sick? Shouldn't we thank God for one another now and not wait until a crisis strikes?

When we look at Jesus, we see a person deeply devoted to prayer. Jesus was connected to the Father every hour, every minute, and every second. His prayers and moments of solitude with God came before all His miracles.

Concluding Thought:

We often treat prayer as a last-ditch effort when things get tough, but it should be our first response. By cultivating a life of prayer, we strengthen our relationship with God and align our hearts with His will. Let's strive to make prayer our first instinct, not just in emergencies, but in all moments of our lives. As we bring everything to God in prayer, we can find peace knowing that He is always near, ready to listen and provide.

Closing Prayer:

Heavenly Father, help me to make prayer a natural and constant part of my life. May I come to You in all situations, not just when times are tough. Strengthen my faith, and remind me that You hear me, care for me, and are always with me. Teach me to rely on You first in all things. In Jesus' name, Amen.

Reflection Questions:

1. How often do you turn to prayer at the beginning of a challenge instead of waiting until later?
2. How can you cultivate a lifestyle of constant prayer and dependence on God?

Scripture for Meditation:

- Thessalonians 5:16-18 (NIV) – "Rejoice always, pray continually, give thanks in all circumstances; for this is God's will for you in Christ Jesus."
- Matthew 6:6 (NIV) – "But when you pray, go into your room, close the door and pray to your Father, who is

unseen. Then your Father, who sees what is done in secret, will reward you."

Week 6: Guarding Against the Ultimate Scam

Have you ever seen someone you care about fall for a scam? I remember a relative of mine who was taken in by a scheme promising quick money. She invested a few thousand dollars, thinking that she would earn even more in return. Instead, she lost everything. The promises that had seemed so sure quickly faded into regret and frustration. It was a heartbreaking lesson in how easily we can be deceived.

Scammers are skilled at telling people what they want to hear and painting pictures of wealth and success. Their tools are lies and manipulation, promising quick rewards that never come. In much the same way, Satan is the ultimate scammer. From the beginning of time, he has lured people away from the truth with deceit, offering them false promises and empty dreams. In John 8:44, Jesus says, *"He (Satan) was a murderer from the beginning, not holding to the truth, for there is no truth in him. When he lies, he speaks his native language, for he is a liar and the father of lies."*

Satan's tactics mirror those of earthly scammers. He presents things that seem too good to be true, tempting us with shortcuts, sinful pleasures, or promises of fulfillment outside of God's will. But just like my relative who believed she would earn thousands of dollars only to end up with nothing, Satan's lies leave us empty and broken.

We must be careful not only to avoid falling for Satan's scams but also to guard ourselves against adopting any attitude of deceit in our own lives. When we trick or manipulate others for our gain, we are acting in a way that reflects the enemy, not Christ. Jesus, on the other hand, is the very embodiment of truth. He says in John 14:6, *"I am the way, the truth, and the life. No one comes to the Father except through me."* Jesus calls us to live with integrity and truth in all we do.

As followers of Christ, we are called to be people of truth, not deception. Just as scammers in business seek to manipulate others for their gain, we must resist the temptation to bend the truth or take advantage of others. It can be tempting to look for shortcuts in life, whether in relationships, finances, or personal growth, but these will always lead us down a path that ends in destruction.

Closing Thought:

Satan is always looking for ways to deceive us, offering promises of quick satisfaction, pleasure, or success that ultimately lead us away from God's truth. But we must remain vigilant and rooted in Christ, who is the truth. When we walk in integrity, we are protected from the enemy's schemes, and our lives reflect the honesty and righteousness of Jesus. Be mindful of the decisions you make and the attitudes you hold, ensuring that you reflect Christ's truth in all things.

Reflection Questions:

1. Have you ever been deceived by something that seemed too good to be true? How did it impact your life?
2. What steps can you take to guard yourself against spiritual scams and lies from the enemy?
3. How can you help those around you who may be struggling with deception or being led astray by false promises?

Scriptures for Meditation:

- **John 8:44** – "You belong to your father, the devil, and you want to carry out your father's desires. He was a murderer from the beginning, not holding to the truth, for there is no truth in him. When he lies, he speaks his native language, for he is a liar and the father of lies."
- **John 14:6** – "Jesus answered, 'I am the way and the truth and the life. No one comes to the Father except through me.'"

Week 7: Grace In Failures

One of the most important lessons I've learned in life, both as an individual and as a pastor, is that failure is to be expected and learned from. I know that failure happens to everyone, but I can only speak for myself. I have misspoken, misstepped, and disappointed others and myself in more ways than I can explain here. To be honest, I admit that failure hurts. It hurts me, and it hurts others. I understand why most of us fear it. We fear failure because we are worried about what others will think of us. We fear what we might lose. Often, failure results from poor judgment or simply the bad execution of an idea. Sometimes, it stems from our selfishness or pride. For some, it may even be a moral failure.

However, I have found that there is much grace to be found in failure—not in the failure itself, but in Christ, who works in us and through us in both our successes and failures. The good news is that God's grace covers everything.

How do we find grace in our failures? While failure pushes us to learn from our experiences and from others, it also brings us to a place of humility. It wakes us up. We are reminded that we still have so much to learn. Failures point us to the One who is truly righteous and holy. God is at work in our lives. We may not have accomplished what we wanted, but God helps us see that He is working His plan in us. Even in our failures, He tells us we are His workmanship, and we belong to Him.

Most importantly, our failures remind us that we are not the Savior. We are not God. We are not the deliverer. Failures teach us this truth. When I was new in ministry, I often played the role of "Mr. Fix-It," thinking I could solve problems better than others. I was wrong. In fact, it was that attitude that led me to fail many times.

Through studying the scriptures, I learned that God does not "fix" us the way we fix things. We are not things to be used. God is not merely concerned with the moment or the temporary, as we often are. He is eternal, and He cares for our eternity. We need saving more than fixing. We need God's help, even in our best efforts. In short, failures teach us that there is a far better way than how we do things. The better way is Jesus Christ, our Lord and Savior.

Yes, we will fail—often. But our failures do not define who we are. We are defined by what Jesus has done on the cross. He saved us from all our failures, sins, and shortcomings. Whatever mistakes we've made, we are still God's beloved sons and daughters.

"Brothers, I do not consider that I have made it my own. But one thing I do: forgetting what lies behind and straining forward to what lies ahead, I press on toward the goal for the prize of the upward call of God in Christ Jesus" (Philippians 3:13-14, NIV).

Concluding Thought:

Failure is not the end. It is a step along the way in our journey with God. Through failure, we learn humility, perseverance, and dependence on Christ. Let us embrace grace in our failures, knowing that Christ defines who we are, not our mistakes.

Closing Prayer:

Father, thank You for Your grace that covers my failures. Help me to see each failure as an opportunity to grow and learn from You. Teach me to rely on Your strength and wisdom instead of my own. Remind me that my identity is not in my successes or failures but in Christ alone. In Jesus' name, Amen.

Reflection Questions:

1. How can failure be an opportunity for growth in your relationship with God?

2. What does it mean to you that your failures do not define you, but Christ does?

Scripture for Meditation:

- Romans 8:1 (NIV) – "Therefore, there is now no condemnation for those who are in Christ Jesus."
- 2 Corinthians 12:9 (NIV) – "But He said to me, 'My grace is sufficient for you, for my power is made perfect in weakness.' Therefore I will boast all the more gladly about my weaknesses, so that Christ's power may rest on me."

Week 8: When We Lose Someone, We Love

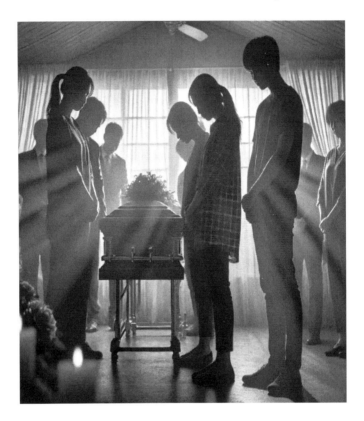

We all have loved ones who have passed away. My mom and dad died several years ago, and yet I still miss both of them.

Each of us will experience the reality of loss—perhaps you already have. And what you remember most about that time is the pain. As life moves on and days turn into nights, you begin to realize that you never truly stop missing that precious loved one. You simply learn to live around the empty space inside you that remains because of their absence.

When we lose someone, we cannot imagine living without, our hearts break, and the truth is that we never completely get over the loss. Because of the love we have for them, we will never forget them.

However, strangely, there is good news. Those we've lost continue to live on in the warmth of our broken hearts, hearts that may never fully heal. Even with our wounds, we continue to grow and experience life.

An analogy that might describe this is like breaking an ankle that never fully heals. After some time, you still feel a certain pain. It hurts when you walk. It hurts when you dance. Yet, you walk and dance anyway, perhaps with a slight limp. This limp adds depth to your life because you realize that life is about more than just pain and suffering. Yes, there is hope. There is joy, even when we limp while dancing.

The people we have lost will remain a part of us. We will remember them and cherish the good moments we shared with them. Most importantly, we look forward to the time when there will be no more pain and tears: *"He will wipe every tear from their eyes. There will be no more death or mourning or crying or pain, for the old order of things has passed away"* (Revelation 21:4, NASB).

Concluding Thought:

Grief is a lifelong process, but so is hope. As we carry the memories of our loved ones, let us also carry the hope of eternal life, knowing that God promises us a future without pain, loss, or sorrow. We may walk with a limp, but we walk in the joy of knowing that we will be reunited one day.

Closing Prayer:

Dear Lord, thank You for the gift of loved ones in my life. As I grieve their loss, remind me of the hope I have in You—that one day, all pain and sorrow will cease. Help me to walk through my grief with grace, knowing that You are with me and that I am not alone. Comfort me in my pain and fill me with the joy of Your promises. In Jesus' name, Amen.

Reflection Questions:

1. How has the loss of a loved one impacted your faith journey?
2. How can the hope of eternal life comfort you in seasons of grief?

Scripture for Meditation:

- **John 11:25-26 (NIV)** – "Jesus said to her, 'I am the resurrection and the life. The one who believes in me will live, even though they die; and whoever lives by believing in me will never die.'"
- **Psalm 34:18 (NIV)** – "The Lord is close to the brokenhearted and saves those who are crushed in spirit."

Week 9: Burglars In the House!

This is something I will never forget while pastoring in San Fernando, Philippines, years ago. All of us in the family were asleep when my wife woke up because she sensed a presence in our bedroom. Her eyes were wide open, and she saw a man in the shadowy darkness of our room. When the man saw my wife was awake, he quickly grabbed her bag near the door. My wife immediately shouted to wake me up and told me that a burglar had entered the house. We quickly shut the bedroom door, locked it, and pushed a heavy dresser to block the entrance.

God, in Every Step

In fear, my wife started shouting so our neighbor across the street could hear us. We heard some scrambling outside our room. The burglars ran out. Our neighbor, who happened to be a policeman, came in with his handgun. But by then, the burglars were gone. He called for backup, and after investigating, they discovered that six burglars had entered our home. They had accessed the house by opening a small window in the kitchen, and a smaller person had opened the back door.

The burglars took almost everything we owned—kitchenware, the television, and even my rubber shoes! And believe it or not, they even stole my Bible! The only thing they left was the piano, which they couldn't carry. The police told us we were fortunate they didn't kill us. In our city, many burglaries result in victims being murdered, especially since most of the thieves are high on drugs. In the room with us were our three children: a five-year-old boy, a three-year-old girl, and a one-year-old baby. We are so grateful that God kept us safe.

When I read the scripture about the thief in the night, I now have a deeper understanding of how sudden and unexpected things can happen without any warning.

The metaphor of the "thief in the night" is a powerful and vivid image used in the Bible to describe the sudden and unexpected return of Jesus Christ. It's not about being a thief but about the unannounced nature of a burglar's arrival. This analogy, found in several New Testament passages, serves as a reminder to believers that the timing of the Lord's return is known only to God. It calls us to stay vigilant, watchful, and spiritually prepared at all times.

God, in Every Step

In our Christian journey, it's easy to fall into complacency. We may begin strong in our faith, eager to follow Christ and live according to His teachings. But as time goes on, the distractions and pressures of daily life can cause us to lose focus. We may drift, becoming more concerned with temporal matters and taking our eyes off eternal ones.

Just as we never expected burglars to break into our homes in the middle of the night, the image of Christ's return as a thief in the night challenges our complacency. Those burglars didn't announce their arrival. They came when we least expected them, catching us unprepared. In the same way, Christ's return will be sudden and unannounced, and those who are not spiritually ready will be left scrambling.

This doesn't mean we should live in fear or anxiety, constantly looking over our shoulders. Instead, it calls us to live with intentionality and purpose, cultivating a life of consistent faithfulness and obedience to God. Jesus warns us in Matthew 24:42, *"Therefore keep watch, because you do not know on what day your Lord will come."*

Our call is to live each day as though Christ could return at any moment. This means staying connected to Him through prayer, studying His Word, and being active in our faith. It also involves regularly examining our hearts to ensure that our lives reflect His love and truth. We must guard against spiritual lethargy, understanding that our walk with Christ is not a sprint but a marathon that requires endurance and vigilance.

"But the day of the Lord will come like a thief in the night. The heavens will disappear with a roar; the elements will be destroyed by fire, and the earth and everything done in it will be laid bare."—2 Peter 3:10 (NIV)

Concluding Thought:

Just as we safeguard our homes, let us safeguard our hearts. Although we do not know the exact date or time, Christ's return is certain and will happen at the precise moment God determines. Stay ready, remain vigilant, and remember that we are called to be faithful in all seasons.

Closing Prayer:

Heavenly Father, thank You for Your grace and protection over us, even when we are unaware of the dangers around us. Help us to stay watchful, to guard our hearts, and to live each day as though You could return at any moment. Strengthen our faith, and keep us grounded in Your Word. In Jesus' name, Amen.

Reflection Questions:

1. Have there been moments in your life where you felt unprepared, spiritually or otherwise? How did that impact you?
2. What are some practical ways you can stay vigilant and spiritually ready for Christ's return?
3. How does the metaphor of Christ's return as a "thief in the night" challenge you in your daily walk with Him?

Scripture for Meditation:

- 1 Thessalonians 5:2 — "For you know very well that the day of the Lord will come like a thief in the night."
- Matthew 24:44 — "So you also must be ready, because the Son of Man will come at an hour when you do not expect him."

Week 10: A Chicken Coop Experience

Several years ago, when my family and I lived in Davao City, on the island of Mindanao, Philippines, we started a small church in the town of Digos. It began with just a few members. We didn't have a grand sanctuary or polished pews—our church rented a small room in an average-looking restaurant for worship services. Many who attended were humble farmers and struggling individuals, living day by day. But in that humble setting, we sought to exalt the Lord together.

One Sunday stands out vividly in my memory. We arrived at the restaurant, only to find that our usual worship room was being used for a wedding. The owner apologized and offered us an alternative worship space. I imagined she would lead us to another room. To my surprise, she directed us to the back of the restaurant—our new worship space was a chicken coop! There were still a few chickens inside. With no other option, we set up our chairs and had our worship service right there, with the chickens clucking in the background.

But what a time we had! There was an unexplainable sense of joy and freedom, worshipping our God in such an unconventional place. We were reminded that God's presence isn't confined to church buildings. He is present wherever His people gather—whether in grand cathedrals or humble chicken coops. That day, God's glory filled that unlikely space, and I believe it was one of the most sincere worship experiences we ever had.

This memory brings to mind the many Christian communities around the world who meet in less-than-ideal circumstances. Some are forced to hide due to persecution, gathering in caves or forests, while others worship under trees or even in garbage dumps. I recall hearing about a man who moved his family into a community built on a garbage dump to live among the people and plant a church. His desire was to bring Jesus' light to the most marginalized. If you are not used to the stench, you might faint upon entering such a place, but to those living there, that dump was their home—and it became a place where God's Kingdom took root.

God's heart has always been with the lowly, the outcasts, and the rejected. It's easy to forget this truth in today's culture, where many seek churches with wealth, prestige, and programs designed for comfort and convenience. But Jesus came for the broken, the poor, and the lost. He said, "It is not the healthy who need a doctor, but the sick… I have not come to call the righteous, but sinners" (Matthew 9:12-13, NIV).

God's calling is not for us to gravitate toward comfort but to see the world through His eyes. When we do, we are drawn to the weak, the sick, and the sinful. We are called to extend our hands to those whom society overlooks. Jesus made His dwelling with the lowly, and He invites us to do the same.

Closing Thought:

The true essence of worship and mission isn't found in comfort or convenience, but in surrendering to God's will, even if it leads us to the unexpected places—the chicken coops of life. In these unlikely spaces, God reveals Himself, and His love is made manifest. Will you step out of your comfort zone to see the world as God sees it?

Prayer Prompt: Lord, help me to see the world through Your eyes. Give me a heart of compassion for the lost, the broken, and the needy. Lead me to serve with humility, just as You came to serve. Whether I'm in a grand building or a humble chicken coop, may my worship be genuine and my heart aligned with Yours. Amen.

Reflection Questions:

1. How does this story of worship in a chicken coop challenge your understanding of where and how worship can happen?

2. Have you ever experienced God in an unexpected or uncomfortable place? How did it impact your relationship with Him?
3. In what ways can you begin to see the marginalized and the needy through the eyes of Jesus in your community?
4. How might you step out of your comfort zone to serve those who are often overlooked by society?

Scriptures for Meditation:

- Matthew 9:12-13 (NIV): "It is not the healthy who need a doctor, but the sick… I have not come to call the righteous, but sinners."
- Isaiah 61:1 (NIV): "The Spirit of the Sovereign Lord is on me because the Lord has anointed me to proclaim good news to the poor."
- Luke 4:18 (NIV): "The Spirit of the Lord is on me because he has anointed me to proclaim good news to the poor. He has sent me to proclaim freedom for the prisoners and recovery of sight for the blind, to set the oppressed free."
- James 2:5 (NIV): "Listen, my dear brothers and sisters: Has not God chosen those who are poor in the eyes of the world to be rich in faith and to inherit the kingdom he promised those who love him?"

Week 11: Delivered Our Baby

There are moments in life that confront us with challenges so intense they test our faith to its very core. For my wife and me, one such moment came when our precious daughter, Carmel, entered the world much earlier than expected.

It was 1988, and we had been sent to the church's Pasadena campus to attend a ministerial refresher course. We were in one of the South Orange Grove apartments.

God, in Every Step

My wife was pregnant, and our doctor had assured us that the baby's birth would be in August. To be safe, we scheduled our attendance at the conference, which began on the first day of June. It was a two-week event, and we expected to be back home by mid-June, ready to prepare for the arrival of our little one. But then, the unforeseen happened.

Late in the evening of June 14th, my wife began to feel pain. Close to midnight, she shook me awake with a sense of urgency in her voice. "The baby may be coming," she whispered. In my ignorance, I naively suggested she lie down with pillows under her, hoping the baby would wait until morning. It was a foolish thought. I soon learned that when a baby decides to come, nothing can stop it!

Realization hit us like a tidal wave—Carmel was arriving early. Fear gripped our hearts as questions flooded our minds. Would she be okay? Would her tiny body be strong enough to survive? We prayed fervently, clinging to the promises of God, yet the uncertainty loomed like a dark cloud over us.

Everything happened so fast. The fear is etched in my memory. At 12:59 a.m., my wife lay down on the shaggy carpet floor, a towel beneath her, and looked at me with a mix of determination and vulnerability. "Bermie," she said, "you need to deliver the baby." I was stunned. Me? Deliver the baby? But there was no time to hesitate. The baby was coming, ready or not.

My wife quickly instructed me. "Get your Swiss knife, cut some of the plastic rope wrapped around that 'balikbayan' cardboard box we planned to take home." My hands trembled as I did as she said, tying a knot on the umbilical cord two inches from the baby and another two inches from her.

As Carmel emerged into the world, I followed my wife's guidance to ensure our baby was safe. Then, I called the doctor we had seen just the day before. After hearing about the delivery and Carmel's condition, he reassured me. "No need to rush to the hospital this early morning," he said. "Just take her and the baby to the clinic later in the morning for a check-up." We did, and by some miracle, both mother and baby were perfectly normal. The father? Well, I was left reeling from the experience.

Fortunately, a student on campus who was a doctor from South Africa arrived when he found out what happened. He was so calm, a stark contrast to my frayed nerves. He helped my wife to ensure that the placenta was delivered properly.

What's the point of all this? Carmel was born premature, weighing just a little over four pounds. She could have fit in a shoebox. The hours surrounding her birth were filled with a mix of emotions—anxiety, fear, and uncertainty.

And then came the moment I will never forget—the first time I held Carmel in my arms. She was so tiny, yet so full of life. Her eyes sparkled, and her little lips curled into a smile that seemed to light up the entire room. It was as if God Himself was smiling through her, assuring us that He had been with us all along, even in the darkest moments. The fear and anxiety melted away, replaced by an indescribable joy and gratitude.

In holding Carmel, I was reminded that God's joy often comes after the storm. The same God who calmed the seas for His disciples brought peace to our hearts amidst our uncertainty. Carmel's smile was a testament to the joy that comes when we trust in God's timing and His perfect plan, even when we don't fully understand it.

Life is filled with unexpected challenges that can shake our faith and cause us to question God's plan. But it is in these very moments that God invites us to draw closer to Him, to trust that His plans for us are indeed for our good, even when they don't align with our own. Carmel's journey has taught me that God's faithfulness is unwavering, and His joy is always on the other side of fear. And yes, that is something I will never forget. I delivered our baby girl.

Concluding Thought:

In our moments of greatest fear and uncertainty, God shows us His love in ways that go beyond what we can imagine. Trusting Him, even in times of difficulty, opens the door to a joy that can only come from knowing He is in control.

Closing Prayer:

Dear Heavenly Father, we thank You for Your faithfulness, even in our darkest hours. Help us to trust You in every circumstance, knowing that Your plans for us are good. Give us strength in our weakness and peace in the midst of our storms. Thank You for being with us every step of the way. In Jesus' name, Amen.

Reflection Questions:

1. Can you recall a time when an unexpected event challenged your faith? How did you see God's hand in it afterward?

2. How can you remind yourself to trust God's plan, even when it doesn't align with your own expectations?
3. What are some ways you can encourage others who are facing uncertain or difficult times?

Scripture for Meditation:

- Jeremiah 29:11 — "For I know the plans I have for you," declares the Lord, "plans to prosper you and not to harm you, plans to give you hope and a future."
- Matthew 8:26 — "He replied, 'You of little faith, why are you so afraid?' Then he got up and rebuked the winds and the waves, and it was completely calm."

Week 12: Beauty From Ashes!

Less than a year ago, more than 30 acres of grass and bushes along our bicycling path were reduced to ashes. As I biked this morning, I couldn't help but notice how things had changed. New vegetation had grown, and flowers were blooming.

After the fire, I remember feeling sad as I saw the blackened landscape dotted with what was left of the charcoaled branches.

But today, I realized something remarkable: even the burnt and scorched land is powerless against an all-powerful God who commands rain from the sky and brings forth new life.

We serve an amazing God. In the ashes of our pain and desperation, new green buds of life begin to sprout. Miracles happen. Soon, we find hope and strength in place of despair and weakness.

Over the years, I've seen this happen many times. Gladness overshadows mourning. On days like today, what was once deep sadness is now overwhelmed by joy and peace.

The reality is that our lives can sometimes be messy. The bitterness of ashes may envelop us. We may stumble and trip over our own hopes and dreams. But what I've come to understand is that when we fall into the very mess we hoped to avoid, we often find God's goodness right there. Being scorched by problems is not permanent.

Perhaps today you find yourself sitting in a heap of ashes, despairing. While our hopes, desires, and plans for our lives are finite, an infinite God who loves us can take our lifeless, bitter ashes and transform them into something new and beautiful. Was not our Lord in the grave, dead for three days and three nights? Yet, He has risen and is now alive!

"To console those who mourn in Zion, to give them beauty for ashes, the oil of joy for mourning, the garment of praise for the spirit of heaviness; that they may be called trees of righteousness, the planting of the Lord, that He may be glorified" (Isaiah 61:3, NKJV).

Concluding Thought:

No matter how messy or broken our lives may feel, God can bring beauty out of the ashes. He takes our pain, our loss, and our hopelessness and turns them into something new and full of life. Let's trust Him to bring beauty from the ashes in our own lives, knowing that He has the power to restore and redeem.

Closing Prayer:

Heavenly Father, thank You for Your amazing ability to bring beauty out of the ashes. When life feels messy and hopeless, remind me that You are working behind the scenes, bringing new life where there was once destruction. Help me to trust in Your power to restore and renew. In Jesus' name, Amen.

Reflection Questions:

1. How have you seen God bring beauty out of the ashes in your own life?
2. What situations in your life currently feel like a heap of ashes that need God's touch?

Scripture for Meditation:

- **Romans 8:28 (NIV)** – "And we know that in all things God works for the good of those who love Him, who have been called according to His purpose."

- **2 Corinthians 5:17 (NIV)** – "Therefore, if anyone is in Christ, the new creation has come: The old has gone, the new is here!"

Week 13: God, Are You There?

I must admit that there have been times when I felt God had abandoned me. You've probably felt the same. Sometimes, in the severity of our trials, we may think that God has forgotten about us. I've had many prayers where I cried out, "God, are You there?"

The psalmist expresses a similar sentiment but comes to a comforting realization in *Psalm 139:7-12 (NIV)*: *"Where can I go from your Spirit? Where can I flee from your presence? If I go up to the heavens, you are there; if I make my bed in the depths, you are there. If I rise on the wings of the dawn, if I settle on the far side of the sea, even there your hand will guide me, your right hand will hold me fast. If I say, 'Surely the darkness will hide me and the light become night around me,' even the darkness will not be dark to you; the night will shine like the day, for darkness is as light to you."*

King David's psalms reveal that God will never lose sight of us. There is no place we can go where we are lost to God. We can't go anywhere outside of His knowledge or His watchful care. The scriptures assure us that even in our darkest moments, God is there. Even when we fall into problems, dilemmas, or circumstances where it seems impossibly dark, for God, it is as bright as day. He sees us. He sees us with love.

In other words, you and I may fall into some deep circumstances. We may stumble into some problem or difficult condition, and it feels as though we are surrounded by darkness. But verse 12 reminds us, *"Even the darkness is not dark to You; the night is as bright as the day…"*

As I get older, I find these words to be more and more precious. They remind me of how deeply God cares for us. You and I are precious to Him. He knows us completely. He is involved in our lives, watching over us, guarding us, and protecting us. You and I matter to Him.

Concluding Thought:

No matter how dark or difficult life may seem, God is always there. We are never lost to Him. In our moments of doubt or despair, let's remember that God's light shines brightly, even in our darkest hours. His presence is constant, and His love for us never wavers.

Closing Prayer:

Father, thank You for never abandoning me, even when I feel lost or alone. Help me to trust that You are with me, even in the darkest times. Remind me that I am precious to You and that Your presence is a light that never fades. Give me strength and comfort, knowing that You see me, care for me, and are always near. In Jesus' name, Amen.

Reflection Questions:

1. In what dark moments have you questioned God's presence, and how did He reveal Himself?
2. How can you remind yourself of God's faithfulness when you feel abandoned?

Scripture for Meditation:

- **Isaiah 41:10 (NIV)** – "So do not fear, for I am with you; do not be dismayed, for I am your God. I will strengthen you and help you; I will uphold you with my righteous right hand."
- **Deuteronomy 31:8 (NIV)**

Week 14: Embracing Grief

We have all experienced the pain of losing someone we love. When my dad passed away years ago in the Philippines, I decided to bring my mom to the USA so we could take care of her in her old age. She was 83 at the time. God blessed us with six wonderful years of her living with us. During that time, I had the chance to truly bond with my mom and get to know her better. We shared many meals, countless conversations, and even did some traveling together. It was also a blessing for my four children to connect with their "roots" through their time with their grandmother.

God, in Every Step

When she passed away at the age of 89, I grieved deeply. Even now, I find myself in tears from time to time. I remember a particular moment shortly after her passing. I was in a work meeting when one of my colleagues noticed I looked sad. When he asked me what was wrong, I told him my mom had recently died. Without hesitation, he responded, "Why Bermie, you know there's a resurrection—no need to grieve."

To be honest, his words didn't comfort me. Just because I was grieving didn't mean I had forgotten about the resurrection. My colleague's well-meaning words lacked empathy, leaving me feeling more hurt than supported. He seemed to believe that I needed to "get over" my grief quickly, not understanding that grief isn't something we can just rush through.

Grief is one of the most profound human emotions. Whether we lose a loved one, experience a broken relationship, or endure another deep sorrow, our hearts naturally ache. Yet, society often encourages us to "move on" quickly, as if grief is something we can simply bypass. But rushing the grieving process not only denies the depth of our pain but also stifles the healing work God intends to do within us. Grief, when embraced with patience and empathy, becomes a journey toward healing—not something we can race through.

One of the most crucial reasons we shouldn't rush grief is the need for empathy—for ourselves and others. Grieving deeply allows us to feel the full weight of our loss, acknowledging the value of what or who we've lost. Empathy begins with sitting with that pain and allowing ourselves to experience it. Just as God is patient with us, we must be patient with ourselves and with those around us who are grieving.

When Jesus lost His friend, Lazarus, He didn't rush through His grief. Even though He knew He would raise Lazarus from the dead, He wept. This single verse—*"Jesus wept"* (John 11:35)—reveals the depths of Jesus' compassion. Even knowing the outcome, He took time to mourn, showing that grief has a sacred place in our lives.

By allowing ourselves time to grieve, we cultivate empathy. We become more compassionate toward others who are grieving. Instead of offering quick-fix solutions, we can offer our presence and understanding, embodying Christ's love.

Scripture tells us that there is an appropriate time for every emotion and experience under the sun. In Ecclesiastes 3:4, we are reminded, *"There is a time to weep and a time to laugh, a time to mourn and a time to dance."* Grieving is part of the rhythm of life. We must not rush through the weeping and mourning, for these moments are as sacred as times of laughter and joy.

When we rush through grief, we rob ourselves of the full emotional range God has given us. In His wisdom, God created time and seasons for every experience. It's okay to not "be okay" immediately after a loss. We should allow ourselves the space to weep, knowing that this process will eventually lead to healing. I have a brother who passed away a few years ago, and grief still comes to me now and then—not because I don't believe in the resurrection, but because I loved him deeply and miss him.

In His Sermon on the Mount, Jesus spoke these comforting words: *"Blessed are those who mourn, for they will be comforted"* (Matthew 5:4). Here, Jesus is not telling us to avoid or diminish our grief but to embrace it. It is through mourning that we receive comfort from God. There is a blessing in mourning because it opens the door for God's healing presence in our lives. Rushing the process can block the deep comfort that God longs to pour into our hearts.

Grief is not just an emotional response but also a spiritual one. It opens us up to God's comfort in ways that joy never could. By staying in our sorrow for a time, we create space for God to minister to our brokenness.

Healing doesn't mean forgetting. It means learning to live with the loss and finding peace in God's presence amid it. Often, grief exists because of love.

We can be encouraged by the words of Psalm 34:18, *"The Lord is close to the brokenhearted and saves those who are crushed in spirit."* God meets us in our brokenness and walks with us through the valley of sorrow. In these moments, He draws us nearer to Him, using our grief to deepen our relationship with Him.

Concluding Thought:

Grief is not a process we can rush through or avoid. It is a sacred journey that, when embraced with patience, allows God to work healing in our hearts. Let's remember that mourning is not a sign of weakness or a lack of faith but a profound expression of love. In time, God's comfort will come, and we will find peace in His presence.

Closing Prayer:

Loving Father, thank You for Your compassion and patience as we walk through seasons of grief. Help us to embrace the process of mourning, knowing that You are with us every step of the way. Teach us to be empathetic to ourselves and others, and may we experience the deep comfort that only You can provide. In Jesus' name, Amen.

Reflection Questions:

1. How have you experienced grief in your own life, and what has helped you navigate through it?
2. In what ways can you offer empathy to someone who is grieving?
3. How can you invite God into your grieving process to experience His healing presence?

Scripture for Meditation:

- *John 11:35* – "Jesus wept."
- *Psalm 34:18* – "The Lord is close to the brokenhearted and saves those who are crushed in spirit."
- *Matthew 5:4* – "Blessed are those who mourn, for they will be comforted."

Week 15: Tax Day

For those who live in the USA, we know that April 15 is a day to remember. It's the deadline to file our income taxes. My wife and I have always done our best to ensure enough withholding taxes are taken so that we don't have to pay additional tax during filing.

But recently, it happened that we must pay more tax. We pay federal tax, state tax, sales tax, property tax, and so on. There is nothing much we can do. The government wants more of our money. The harder you work to earn a higher income, the higher your income tax will be.

In our journey through life, we encounter numerous paths. One significant crossroad is our relationship with money. It's easy to fall into the trap of using money as a measure of our worth or comparing ourselves to others based on material possessions. However, the wisdom found in **Matthew 6:19-21** reminds us of a profound truth: true wealth transcends earthly treasures.

"Do not store up for yourselves treasures on earth, where moths and vermin destroy, and where thieves break in and steal. But store up for yourselves treasures in heaven, where moths and vermin do not destroy, and where thieves do not break in and steal. For where your treasure is, there your heart will be also."

Jesus teaches us to shift our focus from accumulating possessions that are temporary and prone to loss to investing in eternal treasures. Earthly wealth can vanish in an instant, but the treasures stored in heaven endure for eternity. Our heart's allegiance follows our investments. When prioritizing heavenly treasures—such as love, kindness, generosity, and spiritual growth—our hearts align with God's kingdom values.

Finding true wealth involves understanding that material possessions, while enjoyable, do not define our identity or bring lasting fulfillment. Instead, it's the intangible aspects of life—relationships, experiences, and our connection with God—that enrich our souls and bring enduring joy.

As you navigate the complexities of managing money, remember the importance of aligning your financial decisions with your values and faith. Seek to use money as a tool for good. Strive to cultivate a heart that treasures what is eternal and invest in the things that truly matter in God's kingdom.

Concluding Thought:

True wealth is not found in material possessions but in the eternal treasures we store in heaven. As we prioritize the things that matter to God, we experience lasting joy and peace that the world cannot offer.

Closing Prayer:

Lord, help me to focus on what truly matters in life. Guide me to invest in relationships, acts of kindness, and spiritual growth that store treasures in heaven. Teach me to manage the resources You've given me with wisdom and to use them for Your glory. In Jesus' name, Amen.

Reflection Questions:

1. How can you shift your focus from earthly wealth to heavenly treasures?
2. What steps can you take to align your financial decisions with your faith and values?
3. In what ways can you invest in relationships and acts of generosity in your community?

Scripture for Meditation:

- Matthew 6:19-21 — "For where your treasure is, there your heart will be also."

• Luke 12:15 — "Then he said to them, 'Watch out! Be on your guard against all kinds of greed; life does not consist in an abundance of possessions.'"

• Proverbs 3:9-10 — "Honor the Lord with your wealth, with the first fruits of all your crops; then your barns will be filled to overflowing, and your vats will brim over with new wine."

Week 16: Disappointments

We all experience disappointment—it comes in many forms. It might be an unexpected phone call from the doctor, bad news from an election, or the loss of a job. Disappointment has the power to rob us of our joy and peace if we let it.

Even Elijah, the great prophet who called down fire from heaven, faced deep disappointment. After his victory over the false prophets in 1 Kings 19, he received a death threat from Queen Jezebel. In fear and disappointment, he fled and prayed to God to take his life, feeling utterly defeated and alone.

But God didn't leave Elijah in his despair. Instead, God reminded him that he wasn't alone and that there were thousands of others standing with him. Elijah had lost sight of the bigger picture. Like Elijah, we often overreact when we focus solely on our pain and forget God's plans for us.

When we allow disappointment to consume us, it becomes easy to focus only on ourselves. We withdraw, feeling as though life is unfair, and we forget that God is bigger than the moment we are stuck in. God doesn't focus on moments—He sees the entirety of our lives and His eternal plans for us.

When God came to Elijah, He didn't appear in the wind, the earthquake, or the fire. He came in a gentle whisper. When we're caught up in disappointment, we need to quiet our hearts to hear God's voice. He's still with us, ready to guide us back on track.

Don't let disappointment steal your destiny. Instead, turn to God, trust Him, and listen for His whisper. He will help you come out of the cave of self-pity and into the light of His purpose for your life.

Concluding Thought:

Disappointment is inevitable, but how we respond to it makes all the difference. By trusting God and listening to His voice, we can overcome disappointment and continue moving forward in His plans for us.

Closing Prayer:

Lord, when disappointment overwhelms me, help me to remember that You are with me. Help me to hear Your voice, trust Your plan, and move forward with faith. Guide me out of self-pity and into the fullness of Your purpose for my life. In Jesus' name, Amen.

Reflection Questions:

1. How have you allowed disappointment to affect your relationship with God?
2. How can you remind yourself of God's faithfulness when facing disappointment?

Scripture for Meditation:

- **1 Kings 19:11-12 (NIV)** – "The Lord said, 'Go out and stand on the mountain in the presence of the Lord, for the Lord is about to pass by.' Then a great and powerful wind tore the mountains apart and shattered the rocks before the Lord, but the Lord was not in the wind. After the wind, there was an earthquake, but the Lord was not in the earthquake. After the earthquake came a fire, but the Lord was not in the fire. And after the fire came to a gentle whisper."
- **Isaiah 41:10 (NIV)** – "So do not fear, for I am with you; do not be dismayed, for I am your God. I will strengthen you and help you; I will uphold you with my righteous right hand."

Week 17: A Moment of Peace In Diversity

  Last Tuesday night, I went to the Los Angeles airport to pick up my wife and son, David, from their week-long vacation in New Jersey. I knew they'd be hungry by the time they arrived, so I stopped by David's favorite spot—In-N-Out, the famous burger joint near the airport. I ordered a "double-double" for him, a regular burger for my wife, and of course, a burger for myself as well (smile). I ordered the sandwiches to go. Shortly after, I received a text from David saying that their plane had landed but that it would take some time for them to disembark. With so many flights coming in, I had to wait.

God, in Every Step

There weren't any empty tables, so I grabbed a seat on a stool by a raised table. I sat there for almost an hour before my wife called to say they were finally exiting the plane.

But what stood out to me during that hour wasn't just the wait. It was the people I saw in the restaurant. From my seat, I had a good view of everyone. To my left was a Hispanic family with three children, happily enjoying their burgers and fries. A little further away was a couple with a giggling baby. To my right was a Black family, with the grandparents smiling as they shared their meal together. The restaurant looked like a microcosm of the Los Angeles community. I saw Asians, Armenians, Koreans, and people whose backgrounds I didn't recognize.

Everyone looked happy, savoring their meals. A few minutes later, two white police officers came in and stood in line for their food. Despite the differences in ethnicity, background, and age, the joyful atmosphere didn't change. We were all there together laughing, eating, and enjoying the moment.

For many, this might seem like just a small, ordinary moment. But for me, it was profound. In that diverse crowd, there was unity, peace, and happiness. It struck me how much the world could benefit from moments like this. If only more people could see what I saw—a motley group of individuals, united in their simple enjoyment of life.

That moment made me think: if we are intentional about looking for these little moments of love, peace, and joy in everyday life, we may find hope for the bigger things. It reminded me that in our diversity, we truly can live together peacefully. Perhaps, under God's loving guidance and care, small moments like this can spark healing in our land.

Concluding Thought:

Peace is possible, even in a world full of diversity. If we take time to notice the little moments of joy and unity around us, we may begin to see the path toward healing. God's love transcends all differences, and it's in these everyday moments that we can glimpse His kingdom here on earth.

Closing Prayer:

Lord, thank You for the moments of peace and joy that remind us of Your love. Help us to notice and appreciate the small signs of unity and harmony around us. May we carry this peace into our own lives and share it with others, trusting in Your guidance to heal the brokenness in our world. In Jesus' name, Amen.

Reflection Questions:

1. When was the last time you experienced a moment of unity in diversity?
2. How can you be intentional about noticing the small moments of peace in your daily life?

Scripture for Meditation:

- **Ephesians 4:3 (NIV)** – "Make every effort to keep the unity of the Spirit through the bond of peace."

- **Romans 12:18 (NIV)** – "If it is possible, as far as it depends on you, live at peace with everyone."

Week 18: Traveling Light

Traveling. It's a passion that ignites my soul. My recent experience of exploring the diverse landscapes of the Philippines not only opened my eyes to new wonders but also taught me an invaluable lesson along the way.

As I journeyed through various tourist spots, I couldn't help but notice fellow travelers struggling under the weight of their oversized suitcases, held together by makeshift ropes or packing tape. In today's world, airlines seem to charge a premium for every additional ounce of luggage, turning what should be an adventure into a burdensome ordeal.

But amidst this chaos, I made a conscious decision to embrace light travel. I chose to be a backpacker. I ditched the cumbersome suitcase in favor of a sleek backpack, and in doing so, I uncovered a newfound freedom.

Interestingly, traveling light isn't just about shedding physical weight; it's a metaphor for life itself. How often do we carry unnecessary burdens—worries, regrets, unforgiveness, and resentments—that weigh us down?

The ancient wisdom of casting our cares upon a higher power resonates deeply in this context, urging us to release the baggage that holds us back. Jesus tells us in Matthew 11:28-30 to come to Him, all who are weary and burdened, and He will give us rest. His yoke is easy, and His burden is light. In Him, we find the freedom and peace we long for when we surrender our heavy loads.

Concluding Thought:

Just as traveling light allows us to move freely and enjoy the journey more fully, letting go of life's burdens helps us experience the fullness of life that God intends for us. Why carry unnecessary weight when Christ invites us to leave our cares with Him?

Closing Prayer:

Lord, thank You for inviting us to cast our burdens on You. Help us to release the things that weigh us down—worry, regret, bitterness, and fear. Teach us to trust You completely and to walk through life with a light heart, confident that You carry us through every challenge. In Jesus' name, we pray. Amen.

Reflection Questions:

1. What burdens are you currently carrying that you need to surrender to God?
2. How can you embrace the freedom of "traveling light" in your spiritual journey?
3. How does trusting in God's care change the way you approach life's challenges?

Scripture for Meditation:

- 1 Peter 5:7 — "Cast all your anxiety on Him because He cares for you."
- Matthew 11:28-30 — "Come to me, all you who are weary and burdened, and I will give you rest. Take my yoke upon you and learn from me, for I am gentle and humble in heart, and you will find rest for your souls."

Week 19: Jesus, Our Tap Card

Many are familiar with using tap cards to ride the train or bus. For me, it was an entirely new experience. When I visited my son, Ben, and his family in Alexandria, Virginia, I realized that visiting the Smithsonian Museums in DC wasn't as easy as I had hoped. Traffic was heavy, and finding parking was challenging.

My son suggested that I try using the DC Metro rail. At first, I was hesitant because I wasn't familiar with it. But with each subsequent use, travel became more convenient and enjoyable. I quickly became accustomed to using a tap card for the trains.

When I returned home, I decided to get my own tap card and explore Los Angeles County. There are so many places I want to visit, including museums, parks, the Central Library, and even Long Beach! I'm sure many readers who are daily commuters can relate to using tap cards.

This small, convenient card is essential for travel—it grants us entry and ensures we reach our destination. Without it, we're stuck at the gate, unable to board, no matter how eager we are to continue.

Similarly, in our spiritual journey, Jesus Christ is our "tap card." He grants us access to the Kingdom of God. Just as we cannot board a bus or train without a tap card, we cannot enter the Kingdom of God without Jesus.

The tap card is a necessary prerequisite for our travels. It holds the codes required for our journey. Without it, we cannot proceed. In the same way, Jesus is our essential access to eternal life. He paid the price for our sins through His death and resurrection, and by accepting Him, we hold the key to salvation.

John 14:6 (NIV) reminds us: *"I am the way and the truth and the life. No one comes to the Father except through me."* Just as the tap card is the only way to board the train, Jesus is the only way to enter the presence of God.

There's a sense of assurance when we tap our card at the gate. We know we're allowed to board and continue our journey. In the same way, with Jesus, we have blessed assurance. He promises never to leave or forsake us (Hebrews 13:5). With Him, our path is secure, and our destination is guaranteed.

Tap cards often work across different transportation systems within a city. In a similar way, Jesus' sacrifice is universal—offering salvation to all who believe, regardless of background or past. Romans 10:13 (NIV) says: *"Everyone who calls on the name of the Lord will be saved."*

Some may find the metaphor of Jesus as a tap card unusual. But Jesus Himself often used metaphors. He said He is the door. While we don't take these images literally, they help us understand His role in our lives. Like a tap card, Jesus grants us access to eternal life.

When Jesus gave His life for humanity, we were given a spiritual "tap card" that grants us access to God. The difference is that Jesus paid for it, and it has no expiration date. Through Him, we are invited on a journey to a place of eternal joy and beauty where there are no more pain, suffering, or tears.

As you go about your day, every time you use your tap card, let it remind you of Jesus' role in your life. He is your access, your assurance, and your constant connection to the Father. Embrace this truth and continue your spiritual journey with confidence and gratitude.

Concluding Thought:

Just as a tap card grants us access to our physical destinations, Jesus grants us access to eternal life. With Him, our journey is assured, and our destination is secure. Let's embrace the truth that Jesus is our way to the Father.

Closing Prayer:

Heavenly Father, thank You for sending Jesus to be the way, the truth, and the life. Help me to trust in Him as my access to Your Kingdom. May I live each day with the assurance that You are guiding my journey. Thank You for the gift of salvation through Jesus. In His name, Amen.

Reflection Questions:

1. How does thinking of Jesus as your "access" to God change your perspective on your spiritual journey?
2. In what ways can you grow in your trust and reliance on Jesus as your guide to eternal life?

Scripture for Meditation:

- **John 14:6 (NIV)** – "I am the way and the truth and the life. No one comes to the Father except through me."
- **Romans 10:13 (NIV)** – "Everyone who calls on the name of the Lord will be saved."

Week 20: God's Heart For The Strangers

Sometimes people ask me who my favorite child is. Of course, I love all my children equally. However, there are times when this love is misunderstood.

Let me explain. As a parent of four children, when one of them is in pain or crisis, it's not difficult for my wife and me to focus on the one who is suffering. This special attention does not mean we love our other children any less. It simply means that the child in need requires our immediate care. In the same way, I believe Jesus consistently gives priority to those who are hurting, alienated, and without much hope.

God, in Every Step

Throughout God's story, those on the margins are central to His love and concern. Some may react strongly to the idea that God might have an exclusive love for certain people. But just as I love all my children, the Bible tells us that God is our Father, and John 3:16 makes it clear that God cares for all humanity—no exceptions, no favoritism.

I find it significant that Jesus entered the world as a Galilean Jew. God could have chosen to incarnate Himself among the religious or political elites, but instead, He chose to come into the world as part of a marginalized group. Born to a teenage mother, Mary, and her fiancé, Joseph, who had to flee their home to escape persecution, Jesus' early life mirrors the struggles faced by many today. They experienced the scandal, the uncertainty of displacement, and the difficulty of finding shelter.

If you are familiar with the Gospels, you will see that Jesus' ministry consistently centers on those who are marginalized: the widow, the lame, the poor, the stranger, and the rejected. Interestingly, when He ministers to the rich and powerful, like Zacchaeus, He points them toward a redemptive path that includes making things right with the poor. Jesus' mission was not one of condemnation but of salvation, as stated in John 3:17: *"For God did not send His Son into the world to condemn the world, but to save the world through Him."*

Jesus also sends us into the world to make disciples, never to condemn but to be part of God's saving and redemptive work.

His teachings emphasize the importance of including those on the margins. When you host a feast, Jesus says, invite the outsiders, the broken, and the sinful. The kingdom of God is like a banquet for those who are usually left out. The question for us is, "Do we live this out?"

In Matthew 25, Jesus makes a powerful statement: when we care for the neglected, rejected, and marginalized, we are caring for Him. Jesus laid down His life at Golgotha, a place outside the city gates where criminals were executed, to show that no one is beyond redemption. He sacrificed not only His life but also His reputation so that everyone could understand that they are included in His kingdom.

As I reflect on Jesus' crucifixion, I think of how He was mocked and insulted by the crowds. In Luke 22:65 (NLT), it says they hurled all sorts of insults at Him.

There are groups in our society today—like undocumented immigrants—who are often looked down upon and insulted. I understand that immigration laws exist and should be followed. However, as a former immigrant myself, it grieves me to see prejudice and insults directed at men, women, and children who have been hired, used, and often abused by our economic system in need of cheap labor. These people, created in the image of God, deserve dignity, yet are often treated with scorn, even by those who claim to follow Christ.

Religious people sometimes emphasize the legality of immigration over the grace of Jesus. But where is Jesus' heart in all of this? Would He turn away the stranger? No. Jesus' ministry was always focused on grace, forgiveness, and inclusion.

His death on the cross makes this clear: No one is beyond the reach of God's love. His forgiving grace is extended to all, regardless of our past. The entire story of God's redemptive plan is Good News to the poor, the stranger, and to all believers redeemed by the radical, unconditional love of Jesus.

Concluding Thought:

God's love extends to everyone, especially those on the margins of society. Jesus' life, death, and resurrection show us that no one is beyond redemption. Let us embrace this truth and extend His grace to those who are often overlooked or rejected.

Closing Prayer:

Lord, thank You for Your love that reaches the margins. Help me to see people as You do, with eyes of compassion and grace. May I be a reflection of Your love to those who are hurting, rejected, and in need of hope. In Jesus' name, Amen.

Reflection Questions:

1. How can you demonstrate the love of Jesus to those who are marginalized or rejected in society?
2. What does it mean to you that Jesus laid down His life for those on the fringes?

Scripture for Meditation:

- **Matthew 25:40 (NIV)** – "The King will reply, 'Truly I tell you, whatever you did for one of the least of these brothers and sisters of mine, you did for me.'"
- **John 3:17 (NIV)** – "For God did not send His Son into the world to condemn the world, but to save the world through Him."

Week 21: Nothing Too Small

I recently had a conversation with someone who was feeling a little discouraged because he thought that God didn't really care about him. He believed that God only works with great people on great projects. He felt like he could never attain the faith of Abraham, David, or the apostle Paul. In his mind, God seemed so far away.

But that is not the God of the Bible. Scripture tells us that God doesn't just do the big and amazing things—He also works in the small, everyday moments that might not seem exciting or gain much attention. Some of the coolest things He does happen on regular days, in ordinary places, and through regular people like you and me.

Sometimes, we try to fit God into what we think He should be like, expecting Him to only do grand, unbelievable things. We create boxes for God in our minds, hoping He fits neatly inside them. But these boxes limit our understanding of who God really is.

Thinking that God only does the extraordinary is a bit like believing He only cares about the big, important problems. But the truth is, God cares about *everything* in our lives—even the small, ordinary moments. He's with us when we're working, playing, eating, and simply going through our regular days. He cares about you very personally.

Understanding that God is involved in our everyday lives doesn't make Him any less important; in fact, it shows how detailed and caring He is. The same God who did incredible things, like parting the Red Sea, is the One who notices when a little bird is lost or counts the hairs on our heads (Matthew 10:29–30). He knows when we're going through tough times, and He knows when we're simply having a rough morning. Nothing is too small for Him to notice, and He cares about every little thing in our lives—whether big or small.

Concluding Thought:

God is not distant. He is present in both the monumental and the mundane moments of our lives. Let's be encouraged that nothing escapes His notice. He cares deeply about the small details of our days, and He's with us through it all.

Closing Prayer:

Heavenly Father, thank You for caring about every aspect of our lives. Help us to remember that You are not just the God of big, miraculous moments but also the God of our daily, ordinary moments. Teach us to trust in Your care, knowing that nothing is too small for You. In Jesus' name, Amen.

Reflection Questions:

1. Have you ever felt like God only cares about the big things in life? How does understanding that He cares about the small details change your perspective?
2. How can you begin to notice God's presence in the ordinary, everyday moments of your life?
3. What are some areas of your life, big or small, that you need to entrust to God?

Scripture for Meditation:

- *Matthew 10:29–30* – "Are not two sparrows sold for a penny? Yet not one of them will fall to the ground outside your Father's care. And even the very hairs of your head are all numbered."
- *1 Peter 5:7* – "Cast all your anxiety on Him because He cares for you."
- *Psalm 139:3* – "You discern my going out and my lying down; You are familiar with all my ways."

Week 22: When God Wakes You Up

Growing up, I had the mistaken idea that real men don't cry. I no longer believe that. There have been times in my life when I've found myself crying in the middle of the night. Most of these moments occur during conversations with God after midnight. I've cried out so many times that I've lost count. In fact, I think God and I have a standing appointment at around 3:30 in the morning (smile). Somehow, at that time, I just woke up.

God, in Every Step

I learned from a pastor friend years ago that whenever he wakes up in the night, he considers it God waking him up, wanting to talk.

As I've come to know more Christians, I find great comfort in realizing that I'm not the only one who spends sleepless nights in moments of despair.

The other day, I was reading Psalm 77 and found the writer expressing similar feelings: *"I searched for the Lord. All night long I prayed, with hands lifted toward heaven, but my soul was not comforted."* (Psalm 77:2)

Perhaps you've asked these same questions or shared these same doubts?

The Psalmist continues in his despair: *"Has the Lord rejected me forever? Will he never again be kind to me? Is his unfailing love gone forever? Have his promises permanently failed? Has God forgotten to be gracious? Has he slammed the door on his compassion?"* (Psalm 77:7-9)

During times of trials and afflictions—when God seems distant—it's easy to slip into despair and feel as though God has forgotten us. But when we experience great despair and doubt God's faithfulness, we must do as the Psalmist did: RECALL AND REMEMBER what God has done.

"But then I recall all you have done, O Lord; I remember your wonderful deeds of long ago. They are constantly in my thoughts. I cannot stop thinking about your mighty works." (Psalm 77:11-12)

Are you in that place of despair and doubt? Then RECALL AND REMEMBER. Recall all that God has done for His people, as recorded in the Scriptures. Turn to the pages of the Bible and remember all of God's mighty works. Recall how God has worked in your life and in the lives of your loved ones. Remember all the times you knew—without a shadow of a doubt—that God was present and active in your life. Recall God's promises for you and remember how He has faithfully fulfilled those promises.

Remember the hope we have as precious children of God because of His great love, compassion, and faithfulness. The prophet Jeremiah, a man full of distress and worries, wrote these words to encourage us: *"I remember my affliction and my wandering, the bitterness, and the gall. I well remember them, and my soul is downcast within me. Yet this I call to mind and therefore I have hope: Because of the Lord's great love we are not consumed, for his compassions never fail. They are new every morning; great is your faithfulness."* (Lamentations 3:19-21)

In the New Testament, remembrance is just as vital. One of the functions of the Holy Spirit is to help believers remember: *"But the Helper, the Holy Spirit, whom the Father will send in my name, he will teach you all things and bring to your remembrance all that I have said to you."* (John 14:26)

Remembering what God has done for us is foundational for living the Christian life. How can we be forgiving if we forget the pardon of God purchased at Calvary? How can we find the motivation to sacrifice for others if we don't remember Jesus' sacrifice?

So, if you find yourself awake at night and unable to sleep, perhaps God wants to hear from you. Perhaps He wants you to listen. Either way, remembering what God has done through Jesus Christ, and meditating on what God the Father,

Son, and Holy Spirit continue to do, gives us hope for a better future.

Concluding Thought:

In moments of despair, recall and remember all that God has done for you. When you focus on His faithfulness, you will find hope, even in the darkest of times.

Closing Prayer:

Lord, thank You for Your faithfulness in every season of my life. Help me to recall all that You have done and to trust in Your unchanging love and mercy. When I feel distant from You, remind me of Your constant presence and the hope I have in You. In Jesus' name, Amen.

Reflection Questions:

1. What are some of the ways God has shown His faithfulness to you in the past?
2. How can recalling God's work in your life give you hope during difficult times?

Scripture for Meditation:

- **Lamentations 3:22-23 (NIV)** – "Because of the Lord's great love we are not consumed, for his compassions never fail. They are new every morning; great is your faithfulness."

- **Psalm 77:11-12 (NIV)** – "I will remember the deeds of the Lord; yes, I will remember your miracles of long ago. I will consider all your works and meditate on all your mighty deeds."

Week 23: Seeing Jesus in Every Human Being

She was the daughter of an Albanian grocer, and at age 18, she made a decision that would change not only her life but the lives of countless others. She moved to the slums of Calcutta, where she picked up children from garbage dumps—children riddled with disease, poverty, and despair. That young woman was Anjezë Gonxhe Bojaxhiu, now known as Mother Teresa. When asked what inspired her to do such sacrificial work, she replied with a simplicity that pierced through all human excuses: *"I see Jesus in every human being. I say to myself, this is hungry Jesus, I must feed him. This is sick Jesus. This one has leprosy or gangrene…I serve because I love Jesus."*

God, in Every Step

When I first read this quote, it was like someone had turned on a light in the darkest corner of my heart. I had been a Christian for years, but the truth was that I had grown judgmental, self-righteous, and blind to the suffering around me. I remember driving through downtown Los Angeles and seeing the rows of cardboard boxes lining the sidewalks. My mind quickly filled with harsh thoughts: *"These people must have brought this on themselves—drug addicts, criminals, lazy beggars!"* It was easy to justify my indifference and move on.

But then, I came across Mother Teresa's words. Her philosophy of ministry reshaped how I viewed everything— people, ministry, and even myself. She saw Jesus in the faces of the poor, the sick, and the forgotten. She didn't ask why they were in their condition; she only asked, *"How can I serve Jesus in this person?"* Her words began to work in me like a seed, slowly growing into a new vision for life and ministry: *I see Jesus in every human being.*

Now, I see Jesus in places and people I never expected. Let me share what I mean.

I saw Jesus last week. He was wearing blue jeans and an old shirt, working hard at the church building. He was there alone, sweeping up dust from the floor. For a minute, I thought he looked like a regular church member. But it was Jesus—I could tell by the joy in his smile.

I saw Jesus this morning, too. She was in my kitchen, making breakfast for the family. I glanced over and saw my wife, but then I remembered—*that's Jesus.* I could feel Jesus' love in the way my wife served without expecting anything in return.

This afternoon, Jesus was outside cutting the grass in our community. He waved and smiled at everyone driving by. For a moment, I thought it was just the groundskeeper. But no, it was Jesus—no one else waves with that much joy.

And last night, I saw Him again. He was sitting in the street, looking tired and hungry, with eyes full of pain. It looked like another homeless person, but as I got closer, I realized—it was Jesus. The suffering in His eyes, the depth of His loneliness—it was unmistakable.

Jesus is everywhere. He is in the people we often overlook—the ones who serve us, the ones who need us, and even the ones who seem to have nothing left. And then, early this morning, something else happened. I went to the bathroom, looked in the mirror, and a thought came to my mind: *How do I look to the people I meet?* When they see me, do they see Jesus in me? Does my life reflect His love, His compassion, His joy?

Mother Teresa's vision has changed how I see the world. But now, I am challenged by an even deeper question—*do others see Jesus in me?*

Closing Thought:

In every act of love, kindness, or service, we have an opportunity to reflect Jesus to the world. Just as we should look for Jesus in the faces of those around us, let us also live in a way that others see Jesus in us.

Prayer Prompt:

Lord, open my eyes to see You in everyone I meet. Let me not be blinded by outward appearances, but help me see through Your eyes. And Lord, let others see You in me—in my words, my actions, and my heart. Teach me to serve with humility and love, just as You served. Amen.

Reflection Questions:

1. When you interact with people, do you consciously look for Jesus in them? Why or why not?
2. How can you begin to view those in need through the lens of compassion rather than judgment?
3. In what ways can you better reflect the love of Jesus to others in your daily life?
4. Who in your life might be a "hidden Jesus" you've been overlooking, and how can you serve them this week?

Scriptures for Meditation:

- Matthew 25:40 (NIV): *"The King will reply, 'Truly I tell you, whatever you did for one of the least of these brothers and sisters of mine, you did for me.'"*
- Philippians 2:3-4 (NIV): *"Do nothing out of selfish ambition or vain conceit. Rather, in humility value others above yourselves, not looking to your own interests but each of you to the interests of the others."*
- James 2:14-17 (NIV): *"What good is it, my brothers and sisters, if someone claims to have faith but has no deeds? Can such faith save them? Suppose a brother or a sister is without clothes and daily food. If one of you says to them, 'Go in peace;*

keep warm and well fed,' but does nothing about their physical needs, what good is it? In the same way, faith by itself, if it is not accompanied by action, is dead."

- 1 John 3:17-18 (NIV): *"If anyone has material possessions and sees a brother or sister in need but has no pity on them, how can the love of God be in that person? Dear children, let us not love with words or speech but with actions and in truth."*

Week 24: Significance Over Prominence

I've been a part of the Christian church for many years and have heard countless sermons about advancing the Kingdom of God (including some I've given myself!). These sermons often come with the encouragement for church members to take on something big and radical for God.

Now, don't get me wrong—there are indeed people called by God to do great things in the eyes of others. But it's a serious mistake to suggest that every work of God has to be something spectacular. This kind of thinking sneaks into our egos, inflating our expectations and ambitions, and can lead to monstrous outcomes. The push toward "big" often creates supersized egos, unrealistic expectations, and plans that might make sense only to those caught up in their grandeur.

Talk to some believers who want to "shake the world for God." One or two will have really big dreams, and their plans might involve reaching millions, building mega-churches, or having access to their private jet. But is that what God calls all of us to?

Maybe that's not the path God has for most of us. The idea that only large, grand projects are worthy of God's work can make the average Christian feel inadequate. It can lead those in small churches to feel as though God has forgotten them. That thinking is totally wrong.

Remember that Jesus worked with only twelve disciples. It started small. Yet, through that small group, God built congregations all over the world—many of which remain small. They may not be prominent, but in God's eyes, they are all significant. Both small and large churches make up the entire Body of Christ. Not all are prominent, but all are important.

There are many significant things in life that aren't prominent at all. Think about it: Our eyes are more visible than our lungs, but we can live without our eyes. My hands are more noticeable than my liver, but I can't live without my liver.

What if the small, hidden things in life are just as significant—if not more—than the big, obvious things?

Perhaps that's what God is trying to teach us—He values significance over prominence. Maybe the greatest gift the

Church has to offer the world isn't our big leaders, big buildings, or big talents, but the simple, everyday people of God who are committed to following Jesus faithfully.

What if the church doesn't need another Billy Graham, Mother Teresa, or Rick Warren? What if the church needs more of you—average people like me, committed to walking with Jesus wherever He leads?

Scripture teaches that we were created to fit exactly where God wants us, for specific places, at specific times, to reach specific people (see Acts 17:26).

What if God's life was meant to be revealed through the ordinary, everyday lives of His people? The author Dallas Willard once wrote, "The obviously well-kept secret of the 'ordinary' is that it is made to be a receptacle of the divine, a place where the life of God flows."

Maybe what God is asking from us is not great ability but simple availability. If Jesus could feed thousands of people with just a few pieces of bread and fish, imagine what He can do with whatever we have when we surrender it to Him (Luke 9:16). More than our talents, God desires our faithfulness— our willingness to follow Him wherever He leads.

Concluding Thought:

God calls each of us to a life of significance, not necessarily prominence. What matters is not the size of our accomplishments, but our faithfulness to follow Jesus wherever He leads us. Your ordinary life, in God's hands, can become extraordinary.

Closing Prayer:

Dear Heavenly Father, thank You for reminding me that I don't have to do something grand or spectacular to serve You. Help me to be content with the significance of the work You've given me. Use my life, my talents, and my heart in any way that brings You glory. Teach me to trust that You can do great things with whatever I offer You. In Jesus' name, Amen.

Reflection Questions:

1. How can you shift your focus from prominence to significance in your life and ministry?
2. What are some "ordinary" ways you can serve God that might have a lasting impact?

Scripture for Meditation:

- Acts 17:26 (NIV) – "From one man he made all the nations, that they should inhabit the whole earth; and he marked out their appointed times in history and the boundaries of their lands."
- Luke 9:16 (NIV) – "Taking the five loaves and the two fish and looking up to heaven, he gave thanks and broke them. Then he gave them to the disciples to distribute to the people."

Week 25: Better Than A Map

As my brother and I embarked on our journey to El Nido, Palawan, the Philippines, I felt a surge of excitement. Consulting Google for insights, I eagerly studied the city map, discovering that our hotel was conveniently located near colorful stores, tantalizing restaurants, and just a stone's throw away from the breathtaking beach!

On our second day, at around 7 pm when the sky was dark, we decided to immerse ourselves fully in the experience of being tourists. The bustling streets welcomed us with a multitude of visitors from mostly European nations.

As we strolled along the main thoroughfare, a radiant glow caught my eye on a side street to our left. Intrigued, we ventured forth, finding ourselves amidst a culinary wonderland! Of course, for me as a foodie, that was a great discovery.

The entire street was transformed into a bustling gastronomic paradise, illuminated by twinkling lights and filled with the savory aroma of freshly grilled seafood—fish whose names I don't even know. It was a feast for the senses, and without hesitation, we indulged in its delights for two consecutive evenings.

Reflecting on this unexpected discovery, I realized a profound truth: while maps may guide us, they can never fully capture the essence of a place. Streets may close, intersections may alter, but it is through firsthand experience of walking the streets that we truly grasp the heartbeat of a city.

In much the same way, life unfolds beyond the confines of our initial plans and expectations. Like a map, our beliefs and ideologies may offer guidance, but they are mere interpretations of reality. True understanding comes from embracing the unpredictability and richness of the journey itself.

In our spiritual quest, the Bible serves as our map, directing us to the ultimate truth—Jesus Christ. Yet, it is only through a personal encounter with Him that we uncover the depths of spiritual fulfillment. When we surrender to His presence within us, we unearth a paradise far greater than any earthly map can delineate—a paradise found in the transformative power of His love and grace.

Concluding Thought:

Our journey through life and faith isn't about simply following a map but about engaging deeply with the experiences that shape us. As we encounter Christ personally, we are drawn into a relationship far richer than any set of instructions or plans could ever offer.

Closing Prayer:

Heavenly Father, thank You for guiding us through the journey of life and faith. Help us to embrace the richness of each moment, knowing that Your presence brings true understanding. May we seek not only to follow paths but to encounter You personally along the way. In Jesus' name, Amen.

Reflection Questions:

1. How have unexpected detours in your life led to deeper insights or growth?
2. In what ways can you embrace the unpredictability of life as an opportunity to grow closer to God?
3. How can you cultivate a more personal relationship with Christ beyond simply following religious "maps"?

Scripture for Meditation:

- Psalm 119:105 — "Your word is a lamp to my feet and a light to my path."

- John 14:6 — "Jesus answered, 'I am the way and the truth and the life. No one comes to the Father except through me.'"

Week 26: The Power of Surrender

Perhaps you've heard this story before, but it's worth sharing again because of the powerful lesson it teaches us about surrender.

A group of friends went swimming in a river during the spring when glacier runoff made the water quite dangerous. Despite warnings, one of the friends jumped in, got caught in the current, and was swept away toward the dangerous rapids.

One of the friends on shore was a trained lifeguard. As everyone else panicked, they turned to the lifeguard, urging him to act. But to their shock, he stood still, just watching his struggling friend. The group grew frantic, shouting, "Go save him!" Yet, the lifeguard didn't move.

They watched in horror as their friend continued to fight the current, trying desperately to stay afloat. Then the unthinkable happened—their friend could no longer fight and began to drown. At that moment, the lifeguard sprang into action. With a few swift strokes, he reached the drowning man, pulled him to shore, and saved his life.

Relieved but angry, the group asked, "Why didn't you jump in sooner? He could have died!" The lifeguard responded calmly, "I had to wait until he stopped fighting. If I had jumped in while he was still struggling, he would've dragged me under, and we both would have drowned. But the moment he surrendered, I could safely rescue him."

Isn't this often how it is with us and Jesus? He is always there to save us, but many times we are caught up in the "waters" of life—overwhelmed by problems, heartache, depression, or suffering. We cry out to Him for help, but sometimes it seems like nothing happens. Like the lifeguard, Jesus is waiting for us to stop fighting on our own and fully surrender.

When we finally let go and give up control, He steps in, lifts us out of the waves, and rescues us. In that moment of surrender, we realize that our strength was never enough, but His strength is more than sufficient.

If you are going through a struggle right now, ask yourself: "Am I ready to fully surrender this to God?" It's only when we stop trying to save ourselves that we can truly experience the saving power of Jesus.

Remember this: wherever you are and whatever you're facing, Jesus has a far better plan for your life than you do. He is the perfect King over our lives—loving, wise, and compassionate. No one knows our struggles better than He does, and no one can rescue us as He can.

"The LORD will fight for you; you need only to be still." — Exodus 14:14 (NIV)

Concluding Thought:

Surrender doesn't mean defeat—it means trusting the One who can rescue us. When we stop fighting and let go of control, Jesus steps in and shows us that His grace and strength are all we need. Whatever battle you're facing, trust that God is more than able to bring you through it.

Closing Prayer:

Lord Jesus, help me to stop fighting in my own strength and to surrender fully to You. Teach me to trust You in the midst of my struggles and to rely on Your power to rescue me. I know that You have a plan for my life that is far better than anything I can imagine. Thank You for Your love, Your strength, and Your saving grace. In Your name, I pray, Amen.

Reflection Questions:

1. What area of your life are you struggling to surrender fully to God?
2. How has surrendering to God in the past brought peace or breakthrough in your life?

Scripture for Meditation:

- **Psalm 46:10 (NIV)** – "Be still, and know that I am God; I will be exalted among the nations, I will be exalted in the earth."
- **Matthew 11:28-30 (NIV)** – "Come to me, all you who are weary and burdened, and I will give you rest. Take my yoke upon you and learn from me, for I am gentle and humble in heart, and you will find rest for your souls. For my yoke is easy and my burden is light."

Week 27: The Bible: A Love Story

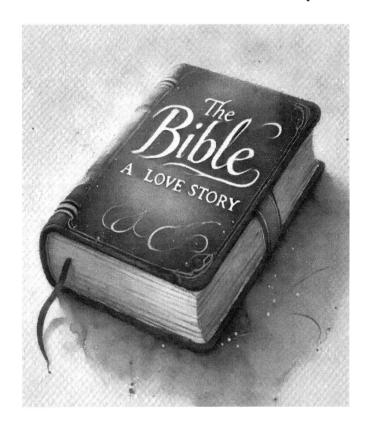

When I first learned about the Bible, I thought it was written to give us rules. In short, I believed the Bible was a rulebook. Some people even think that the word BIBLE stands for "Basic Instructions Before Leaving Earth." But as I grew in my understanding of what the Bible truly is, I realized that it isn't about rules. The Bible is about Jesus (John 20:31).

This book is designed in the context of relationships. The goal of reading the Word isn't about learning the rules; it's about getting to know Jesus—meeting Him along the way and encountering Him personally in our lives. It's about understanding who God is—Father, Son, and Holy Spirit. It's about participating in a relationship, not with a set of doctrines or beliefs, but with the very person of God Himself.

I must admit, this understanding was new to me. What I learned was that some of my so-called "Christian beliefs" were actually misguided, shaped more by worldly religion than by the Word of God.

It's sad to realize that many non-Christians—and even Christians—have misconceptions about what true Christianity is. Many of us think we must behave a certain way to earn God's love, as if we can manipulate Him with our actions. I grew up trying to find ways to please God, thinking He would only love me if I acted "good enough."

We often set up rules for ourselves, believing that they are the key to earning God's approval and love. But when we truly understand the gospel of Jesus Christ, we realize that God loves us despite our behavior. We don't have to work to earn His love. After all, didn't Christ die for us while we were still sinners? (Romans 5:8).

God is love for all eternity. He was love even before time began, and He will always be love. His love for us doesn't depend on what we do or don't do. His love for us is rooted in His nature. The Father, Son, and Holy Spirit love not because of us, but because love is His very being.

Concluding Thought:

The Bible is a love story, not a rulebook. It points us to Jesus, who offers us unconditional love and grace, not because of what we do, but because of who He is. God's love is constant and unchanging. Let's rest in that love and embrace the relationship He offers, rather than trying to earn His affection through our actions.

Closing Prayer:

Heavenly Father, thank You for Your unconditional love. Help me to stop striving to earn Your love and to rest in the truth that You love me no matter what. Open my heart to know You more deeply and to embrace the relationship You offer. May I live my life in response to Your love, not out of obligation, but out of gratitude. In Jesus' name, Amen.

Reflection Questions:

1. Have you ever found yourself trying to "earn" God's love or approval? How can you shift your perspective to embrace His unconditional love?
2. In what ways can you deepen your relationship with God, rather than focusing on religious rules?

Scripture for Meditation:

- **Romans 5:8 (NIV)** – "But God demonstrates his own love for us in this: While we were still sinners, Christ died for us."
- **1 John 4:16 (NIV)** – "And so we know and rely on the love God has for us. God is love. Whoever lives in love lives in God, and God in them."

Week 28: Going On A Vacation

My wife and I are heading on a vacation soon, and I won't reveal the location (smile). We're especially excited because we'll be celebrating our 40th wedding anniversary. The last time we had the chance to properly celebrate our anniversary was our 25th. Since then, life has been so busy with work that we neglected to take time for ourselves, to celebrate and rest. This time, we're eagerly looking forward to this special getaway.

God, in Every Step

I imagine that almost everyone loves vacations, and I'm sure you do too. Summer is just around the corner, and many families and students are looking forward to taking a break from their regular routines—whether from work, school, or daily life. I can picture beaches, mountains, resorts, and entertainment parks filled with people who understand the value of stepping away from the grind to rest and enjoy life.

For many, Monday through Friday is a blur of work, school, or chores. Weekends, instead of being restful, often turn into catch-up days—running errands, attending kids' activities, or keeping up with household duties. Unfortunately, in the rush of life, many have forgotten the importance of dedicating time to worship and fellowship with others.

For my wife and me, this vacation will be a time of rest and refreshment (hopefully!). It will also be a chance for us to rekindle our relationship as husband and wife. More importantly, we're looking forward to taking time to enjoy God's creation and meditate on our relationship with Jesus. After all, true rest is found in Him! We believe that growing in the knowledge of God is a lifelong journey, one that brings peace to our souls and rest to our weary hearts.

Looking back over my own life, I realize that burnout happens when we fill our days with endless activities and forget to walk with Jesus, love Him, commune with Him, and worship Him. Jesus invites us, "Are you tired? Worn out? Burned out on religion? Come to me. Get away with me and you'll recover your life. I'll show you how to take a real rest" (Matthew 11:28-30, MSG).

The Scriptures reveal that God loves giving us the rest we need. Here's an important lesson I've learned: whether it's summer, winter, or any season, to truly achieve the rest we long for, Jesus must be at the center of it. Yes, the beach may be relaxing, and the mountains peaceful, but without the presence of God, they are just temporary stops. It is in His presence that we find lasting peace and rest—even in the midst of life's storms.

"Those who live in the shelter of the Most High will find rest in the shadow of the Almighty." (Psalm 91:1, NLT)

Wherever you choose to vacation this year—whether far away or a simple staycation—be aware of God's presence. It is in the shelter of the Most High that we find the rest that carries us through life. Without Him, weariness will consume us, but with Him, we can live freely and lightly. A true vacation, true rest, is found in Jesus.

Concluding Thought:

Whatever your plans are for rest and relaxation, make sure Jesus is at the center of it. He is the source of true rest and peace. Vacation destinations can be beautiful, but the most meaningful rest happens when we are aware of God's presence, no matter where we are.

Closing Prayer:

Heavenly Father, thank You for the gift of rest. Help us to always find our rest in You, not just in the places we visit or the breaks we take. May Your presence be with us wherever we go, and may we be refreshed in both body and soul. Teach us to slow down and recognize Your hand in our lives, and to make You the center of our rest. In Jesus' name, Amen.

Reflection Questions:

1. When was the last time you truly rested, both physically and spiritually?
2. How can you invite Jesus into your time of rest and refreshment, even in the busyness of life?

Scripture for Meditation:

- **Matthew 11:28-30 (NIV)** – "Come to me, all you who are weary and burdened, and I will give you rest. Take my yoke upon you and learn from me, for I am gentle and humble in heart, and you will find rest for your souls. For my yoke is easy and my burden is light."
- **Psalm 23:1-3 (NIV)** – "The Lord is my shepherd, I lack nothing. He makes me lie down in green pastures, he leads me beside quiet waters, he refreshes my soul."

Week 29: What Is True Beauty?

Today, beauty is often defined by fleeting qualities: smooth skin, sparkling eyes, and strong bodies. We invest enormous amounts of money, time, and energy into preserving this outward appearance, hoping to hold on to youth.

Did you know that global spending on beauty products in 2023 is estimated to be around $571 billion? This includes cosmetics, skincare, haircare, fragrances, and other personal care items. By 2025, it's expected to grow to $716 billion. No matter the source, the estimates are staggering, showing just how much our culture values external beauty.

While there's nothing wrong with wanting to look good and maintain personal hygiene, time remains an unyielding force. No matter how hard we try, age will eventually reclaim what it once lent us. Even the most stunning individual will one day find their once-radiant skin wrinkled, their strong body weakened, and their voice softened. I know this truth personally as I see it reflected in the mirror or when comparing photos from past years.

Sadly, society's definition of beauty is often dictated by movies, social media, and reality TV, creating a narrow standard that many strive to meet. This unrealistic image can leave us feeling inadequate or constantly chasing something we can never fully attain.

But what if we've been searching for beauty in the wrong place all along? As we age, the physical fades, but our inward being—our spirit and our heart—can grow stronger and more radiant. This is the beauty that God values. Unlike external appearance, it doesn't fade but becomes even more precious with time.

The Bible reminds us that true beauty is not found in the outer shell, but in the spirit within. The world celebrates youth, charm, and physical allure, but God treasures a heart that reveres Him. This kind of beauty endures, even when everything else fades away.

My wife and I are now in our 60s, and yet, from my perspective, she is still the most beautiful woman in the world. Even as our bodies age, our spirits continue to bloom, growing more vibrant in wisdom, love, and faith. What truly matters is not what the world sees, but what God sees in us. And He sees far beyond the temporary to what is eternal.

Don't get me wrong. There are valid reasons why people strive to look good. It might be required in the workplace, to boost confidence, help us feel younger, or perhaps it's simply to cover a blemish.

However, while it's good to put effort into our appearance, as we journey through life, let's resist the temptation to place our worth in superficial standards or compare ourselves to Hollywood's version of beauty. Instead, let's focus on cultivating the beauty of the soul. Let kindness, love, and patience flourish within us. In doing so, we reflect a beauty that time cannot steal—a beauty that will last forever.

Concluding Thought:

True beauty is more than skin deep. While the world focuses on outward appearances, God looks at the heart. As we grow older, let us invest in the kind of beauty that matters to Him—a beauty that radiates from a heart full of love, kindness, and grace.

Closing Prayer:

Heavenly Father, thank You for reminding us that true beauty comes from within. Help us to cultivate a heart that honors You, reflecting the love, kindness, and patience that You desire. As we grow older, may our spirits grow more vibrant, reflecting Your grace and wisdom. Help us to see ourselves and others through Your eyes. In Jesus' name, Amen.

Reflection Questions:

1. What standards of beauty do you find yourself influenced by, and how do they affect your self-perception?
2. How can you shift your focus from outward appearance to inner beauty in your daily life?
3. What are some ways you can reflect God's beauty through kindness, love, and grace to those around you?

Scripture for Meditation:

- *1 Samuel 16:7* – "The Lord does not look at the things people look at. People look at the outward appearance, but the Lord looks at the heart."
- *1 Peter 3:3-4* – "Your beauty should not come from outward adornment, such as elaborate hairstyles and the wearing of gold jewelry or fine clothes. Rather, it should be that of your inner self, the unfading beauty of a gentle and quiet spirit, which is of great worth in God's sight."

Week 30: Raising the Spiritually Dead to Life

If I asked you to join me in visiting a local cemetery to raise the dead, you would surely think I'm crazy. You'd probably refuse to go because you and I both know that the dead stay dead.

In church, we often talk about sharing the good news of Jesus Christ. We know God has given us a mission: to make disciples for Christ (Matthew 28:19-20). When it comes to evangelism and disciple-making, I'm reminded of the story where Jesus raises Lazarus from the dead. This powerful story highlights our own desperate condition before a holy God.

Before encountering God, weren't we all spiritually dead? (Ephesians 2:5).

Over the years as a pastor, I've officiated and attended many memorial services. One thing is clear: dead people can't do anything. They can't walk, talk, breathe, or feel. The body stays in the casket, lifeless. The dead cannot tell themselves, "Rise up!" They cannot say, "Breathe!"

In the same way, spiritually speaking, the dead cannot raise themselves to life. This is a crucial point to remember when sharing the gospel. Many non-Christians can become confused when they're told they need to do something to be saved. They hear a list of "do's and don'ts" that suggests God expects them to behave a certain way before granting them life. But here's the truth: just as the dead can't perform any action to revive themselves, spiritually dead people cannot do anything good to receive salvation. It takes the miraculous work of God to raise the spiritually dead to life.

This is where the story of Lazarus comes in as a powerful illustration. Lazarus did nothing to deserve or earn his resurrection. He didn't contribute to it in any way. It was Jesus who called him out of the grave, just as it is Jesus who raised us from spiritual death to life. Salvation isn't about what we can do—it's about what Jesus has already done for us.

So, when we share the gospel, we must remember that it's like raising the dead—it takes a miracle from God. Just as we can't physically raise the dead, we cannot raise the spiritually dead through our efforts. Only Jesus, the Savior of the world, can do that. Our job is to share the good news: Jesus has already saved them. When people believe this truth, it leads them into a relationship with God, one that brings true joy.

Concluding Thought:

Sharing the gospel is like witnessing a miracle. It's not about what we can do, but about what Jesus has already done. Just as Lazarus could not raise himself, neither can we or others come to spiritual life without the power of God. Let's trust in His finished work and share the good news that Jesus has brought us life.

Closing Prayer:

Heavenly Father, thank You for the gift of salvation through Your Son, Jesus. We were dead in our sins, but You raised us to life through the power of Your love. Help us to remember that it's not by our strength or works, but by Your grace that we are saved. Guide us as we share this message of hope with others, trusting that You will work miracles in their lives. In Jesus' name, Amen.

Reflection Questions:

1. Have you ever felt like you were spiritually "dead" before you encountered God's grace?
2. How can you share the gospel message with others in a way that highlights God's miraculous work in raising the spiritually dead?

Scripture for Meditation:

- **Ephesians 2:4-5 (NIV)** – "But because of his great love for us, God, who is rich in mercy, made us alive with Christ even when we were dead in transgressions—it is by grace you have been saved."
- **John 11:25-26 (NIV)** – "Jesus said to her, 'I am the resurrection and the life. The one who believes in me will live, even though they die; and whoever lives by believing in me will never die.'"

Week 31: When Things Go Wrong

How do you react when things go wrong? Perhaps your email or Facebook accounts get hacked, and people send you shocking messages. Maybe your child misbehaves in public, or your teenager makes choices that bother you. You're caught in heavy traffic and are late for an important meeting. Or perhaps someone gossips about you with baseless accusations. How do you respond in these moments?

In situations like these, it's easy to worry about what people think or to get angry with ourselves or others. But we also have the option to surrender these worries to God.

What I'm thinking right now is, *What's done is done.* I can't control how others will react, so I choose to leave it with God and trust Him. This is a spiritual discipline I have found to be incredibly helpful: submitting to the sovereign Lord.

In his book *Renovation of the Heart*, Dallas Willard makes a valuable point—abandoning outcomes to God is essential for our spiritual growth and the care of our souls. This has been extremely helpful to me, and I've seen how transformative it is for others as well. What does it really mean to abandon outcomes to God?

Willard writes, "The secret to peace, as great apprentices of Jesus have long known, is being abandoned to God" (p. 135). He explains further: if grace and wisdom prevail in the life of someone who fully surrenders to God's will, that person will move into complete abandonment to God. The individual no longer holds back anything from God.

When we surrender, we no longer fret over "the bad things that happen to good people." Though hardships and suffering may come, we accept them as part of God's plan for good, as He works in the lives of those who love Him (Romans 8:28). Irredeemable harm does not befall those who live in God's hand (p. 150-151).

Over the years, I've learned that when we truly surrender outcomes to God, we experience both contentment and the opportunity to participate in what God is doing in the world.

This transforms us from mere observers into active participants in God's story. No matter how tragic or chaotic the circumstances, we trust God for the best, knowing that He is the power beyond ourselves and cares for us more than we can imagine.

When we stop relying on our own strength and give our worries to God, we are empowered by His grace. We realize that God is acting generously and powerfully on our behalf. Willard explains this beautifully: "The strongest human will is always the one that is surrendered to God's will and acts with it" (p. 152).

Jesus calls us to this kind of trust in Matthew 11:28-30: *"Come to me, all you who are weary and burdened, and I will give you rest. Take my yoke upon you and learn from me, for I am gentle and humble in heart, and you will find rest for your souls. For my yoke is easy and my burden is light."*

As we entrust ourselves to our faithful Creator, we find great freedom. Let us take on Jesus' humility and meekness, the foundation of all virtues, and find rest from all our worries.

Concluding Thought:

True peace comes when we surrender our circumstances and outcomes to God. He invites us to trust Him fully, and when we do, we experience freedom and rest beyond what we could imagine. Let us abandon our worries and place them in God's hands.

Closing Prayer:

Heavenly Father, thank You for being sovereign over every situation in our lives. Help us to surrender fully to You, trusting in Your perfect will. Teach us to abandon our worries and to trust in Your grace. When we face difficulties, remind us that You are in control, and You are working all things for our good. In Jesus' name, Amen.

Reflection Questions:

1. What situations in your life are you struggling to surrender to God?
2. How does abandoning outcomes to God bring peace to your soul?
3. What does it mean to you to actively participate in God's story?

Scripture for Meditation:

- **Romans 8:28 (NIV)** – "And we know that in all things God works for the good of those who love him, who have been called according to his purpose."
- **1 Peter 5:7 (NIV)** – "Cast all your anxiety on him because he cares for you."
- **Matthew 11:28-30 (NIV)** – "Come to me, all you who are weary and burdened, and I will give you rest."

Week 32: Navigating the Liminal Space

My wife and I have a friend who is moving out of their home and relocating to another state. Our friend shared how challenging this process has been, and I can completely relate. Most of us have faced the stress of moving and dealing with unexpected challenges that feel like curveballs. Recently, I came across a word that perfectly captures this experience— liminal.

Having come from the Philippines and learning English in school, *liminal* is a new word for me. Liminal spaces refer to those in-between moments—the threshold between where we've been and where we're going. It's the time when one door has closed, but the next one hasn't yet opened. It's the space between the "no longer" and the "not yet." These moments can feel unsettling, as we're neither fully here nor fully there. Yet, it's often in these uncertain, waiting times that God does some of His deepest work in us.

I remember feeling this way after I retired, asking myself, "What now? Where do I go from here?" I had asked those questions before, but this time I realized I needed a more concrete answer. So how do we navigate life when we find ourselves in these liminal spaces?

Scripture is full of examples of people living in liminal spaces. Abraham waited for years between the promise of a son and the birth of Isaac. The Israelites wandered in the desert for 40 years, between escaping Egypt and entering the Promised Land. The disciples lived in the tension between the crucifixion and the resurrection. These in-between moments were often marked by uncertainty and waiting, but they were also sacred times when God shaped His people's faith and trust in Him.

When we find ourselves in a liminal space, it's tempting to rush through it, to seek clarity, or to grasp control. But these in-between moments are sacred. They invite us to release our need for certainty and trust in God's timing and His process. In the waiting, we learn to depend on Him more fully. In my own life, these times have often become seasons of prayer, meditation, and seeking wise counsel.

Proverbs 16:9 says, *"In their hearts, humans plan their course, but the Lord establishes their steps."* While we may have plans and hopes for where we want to go, it is God who directs our steps, even when the path seems unclear or undefined. Liminal spaces are not wasted—they're part of the journey. These are often times when God is preparing us for what's next in ways we cannot yet see.

If you find yourself in a season of waiting, uncertainty, or transition, take heart. Though uncomfortable, this space is where God is present, refining, and guiding you. Trust that He is with you, even in the unknown, and that His purposes for you are still unfolding.

As Isaiah 40:31 reminds us, *"But those who wait on the Lord shall renew their strength; they shall mount up with wings like eagles, they shall run and not be weary, they shall walk and not faint."* Embrace the liminal space, trusting that God will lead you forward in His perfect time.

Concluding Thought:

Liminal spaces, though uncomfortable, are sacred times of growth and transformation. They invite us to trust in God's plan, even when we cannot see the whole picture. Instead of rushing through these moments, let's allow God to work in us, strengthening our faith and renewing our hope for what lies ahead.

Closing Prayer:

Father, thank You for being with us in the in-between moments of life. Help us to trust in Your timing and Your plan, even when we don't have all the answers. Teach us to embrace the waiting, knowing that You are at work within us.

Strengthen our faith and guide our steps as we walk through these liminal spaces. In Jesus' name, Amen.

Reflection Questions:

1. Have you ever experienced a liminal space in your life? How did it challenge or shape your faith?
2. In what ways can you trust God more deeply during seasons of waiting or uncertainty?
3. How might embracing the unknown help you grow in your relationship with God?

Scripture for Meditation:

- *Proverbs 16:9* – "In their hearts, humans plan their course, but the Lord establishes their steps."
- *Isaiah 40:31* – "But those who wait on the Lord shall renew their strength; they shall mount up with wings like eagles, they shall run and not be weary, they shall walk and not faint."
- *Psalm 37:7* – "Be still before the Lord and wait patiently for him; do not fret when people succeed in their ways when they carry out their wicked schemes."

Week 33: Coming Out of Fear

In today's world, some call this the "age of terrorism." While some leaders downplay these events, for many affected by these tragedies, they are very real and terrifying. The brutal and publicized killings, shared across TV networks and social media, remind us that something is deeply wrong.

Many nations live in fear. Hearing about thousands of people joining terrorist groups across the globe makes us wonder why nothing seems to be stopping it. Politicians argue, leaders make speeches, yet the violence continues to escalate.

The fear intensifies when the enemy seems to be living among us, threatening our daily lives. While some prepare for defense, most of us continue on, trying to live our lives as though everything is okay.

In this context of terror, Jesus' command to "love your enemies" can seem baffling. How can we love those who seek to harm us? How do we love people who want to destroy our families or take our lives because of our faith? These are hard questions, and it's easy to wonder, "Is it even possible to love our enemies?"

But Jesus' words were not just for an ideal world. They were for us—right here, right now—even in the midst of fear and violence. The Bible reminds us in 1 John 4:18 that "perfect love casts out fear." The more we grow in love, the less room there is for fear.

When we focus on global terrorism, our fear can make us view everyone who looks or sounds different as an enemy. But Jesus calls us to break down those walls and reach out to the people around us, even those who seem like our enemies. Love is the antidote to fear, and Jesus showed us that even in the face of suffering.

While we may never fully understand radical groups like ISIS or al-Qaeda, we can pray for them, as hard as that sounds. After all, the apostle Paul was once a persecutor of Christians before encountering Jesus. If God could transform Paul's life, He can reach others too.

We must also remember our brothers and sisters who are being persecuted around the world. Their faith and courage in the face of danger should inspire us to pray for them and stand with them in solidarity.

Loving our enemies doesn't mean we condone their actions or that we will always live in peace. Sometimes, as history shows, love leads to sacrifice. Jesus loved us so much that He died for us, and many others have laid down their lives for their faith. But our hope is not in the safety of this world—it's in the eternal life that Jesus promises.

Jesus never said, "Love your enemies so they will love you back." He said, "Love your enemies and pray for those who persecute you" (Matthew 5:44). While love may not change others, it can change us. And through that transformation, we can live a life that reflects the grace and love of God.

Concluding Thought:

Even in the face of fear, love is our greatest weapon. Jesus teaches us that love can cast out fear and transform our hearts, even when the world feels dangerous.

Closing Prayer:

Lord, help us to love as You love. Give us the strength to love our enemies, to pray for those who seek to harm us, and to trust You in all circumstances. May Your perfect love cast out our fears, and may we be agents of Your grace and peace in a world that needs it so desperately. Amen.

Reflection Questions:

1. What fears are you holding onto today? How can you invite God's love to replace that fear?
2. How can you actively love someone you consider an "enemy" in your life?
3. What can you learn from Jesus' example of loving and praying for those who persecuted Him?

Scripture for Meditation:

- "But I say to you, love your enemies and pray for those who persecute you, that you may be children of your Father in heaven." — Matthew 5:44-45
- "There is no fear in love, but perfect love drives out fear." — 1 John 4:18

Week 34: Discouraged?

We are all human, and we all make mistakes. No one is perfect. When we mess up, we often feel weighed down with guilt and self-condemnation. I've noticed that many people, perhaps you as well, struggle with these feelings of inadequacy.

Here's what often happens: we see our weaknesses and begin comparing ourselves with others who seem to have it all together. This comparison leads us into a downward spiral of sadness, discouragement, depression, guilt, and shame.

At times, well-meaning people might come to us and say things like, "Just try harder!" or "Get over it!"—expecting that their words will magically make everything better. But we all know that this doesn't work in the long term.

The Bible reminds us of an important truth: "The righteous one falls seven times and rises again, but the foolish fall and do not get back up" (Proverbs 24:16). The use of "seven" in the Bible often signifies completeness, meaning it takes time. This verse tells us that godly maturity doesn't happen overnight. When we fall, God is always there to help us get back on our feet. It also reminds us to be patient with ourselves because growing in wisdom takes time. God is incredibly patient with us. He knows our human limitations and is always ready to pick us up.

Remember the story of Peter walking on water? When he took his eyes off Jesus and focused on the storm, he began to sink. But Jesus was right there to pull him up. This is a picture of God's love and grace in our lives. Even when we fall, God is always ready to lift us.

Are you feeling down or discouraged right now? God is right there with you, ready to help.

Over time, I've learned that the way to avoid becoming discouraged by my own failures is to focus on the loving and gracious Jesus. Jesus perfectly represents God's heart. God is love. He is relational, and He desires us to experience His perfect love.

When we dwell on our mistakes and weaknesses, it's easy to slip into pride without realizing it. We want to be approved of and admired, and when we fall short of that expectation, we punish ourselves for not measuring up. But here's the truth: our worth does not come from our performance, possessions, or what others say about us. Our true value comes from Jesus Christ alone.

So, if you're discouraged, shift your focus to Jesus. Worship God, and in doing so, you step out of the limited, self-centered mindset and into the spacious, glorious Kingdom of God.

Discouragement doesn't come from humility; it stems from pride. When we fall, let us rise and run again. God uses our failures to strip us of self-reliance so that His grace can shine through. His mercy is never-ending, and His grace is always enough.

Don't be discouraged by your faults. God doesn't want us to dwell on them. Instead, He wants us to be aware of His grace and strength. In Christ, we have victory (1 Corinthians 15:57). In Him, there is no condemnation (Romans 8:1). That is the loving God who cares for us.

Concluding Thought:

Mistakes are inevitable, but God's grace is greater. Each time we fall, God is there to lift us up. Let's rely on His strength, not our own, and trust in His loving care.

Closing Prayer:

Lord, I thank You that You are always there for me, even when I stumble and fall. Help me to focus on Your grace and strength, rather than my weaknesses. Lift me up when I feel discouraged and remind me of the love and patience You have for me. Teach me to trust You and walk in Your grace. In Jesus' name, Amen.

Reflection Questions:

1. How do you usually respond when you make mistakes? Do you find yourself focusing more on your failures than on God's grace?
2. What steps can you take to focus more on Jesus and less on your shortcomings?
3. How can you remind yourself of God's promise to pick you up when you fall?

Scripture for Meditation:

- "The righteous one falls seven times and rises again, but the foolish fall and do not get back up." — Proverbs 24:16
- "But thanks be to God! He gives us the victory through our Lord Jesus Christ." — 1 Corinthians 15:57
- "There is therefore now no condemnation for those who are in Christ Jesus." — Romans 8:1

Week 35: The Three-Way Relationship

One of the greatest truths I've learned through the years is this: relationships are foundational in everything related to God and His creation. Whether in families, ministry, marriage, or outreach, relationships matter. The Bible reveals that these relationships aren't just between two people—Jesus is always present as the third person in our relationships. He is the one mediator (1 Timothy 2:5).

God cares deeply about your relationship with Him, but He also cares about your relationships with others. God created us to be relational beings, and He desires to heal the broken relationships that often cause pain in our lives. Many of the troubles we face in the world—wars, corruption, dishonesty—stem from broken relationships.

Lying is wrong because it breaks relationships. Stealing is wrong because it destroys trust. God's design for us is to live in harmony with one another, just as the Father, Son, and Holy Spirit exist in perfect love and unity. When we follow God's lead, our relationships can reflect His love, healing, and grace.

At its core, the Christian life is not about following rules or religious obligations—it's about building relationships. As followers of Jesus, we are called to love one another, even when it's hard. Jesus even tells us to love our enemies (Luke 6:27). Why? Because God loves them too. When we love those who are difficult to love, we reflect God's heart for the world.

In this broken world, God invites us into His love, into His mission of reconciliation. He calls us to be bridge builders, creating connections and loving relationships that reveal His grace. This is the heart of true ministry—caring for others as God cares for us.

Concluding Thought:

God desires for us to participate in His love by building and restoring relationships. As we allow Jesus to be the center of our relationships, we reflect His grace and compassion to the world. Let us live out this calling by loving one another, even in difficult circumstances.

Closing Prayer:

Lord, help me to love as You love. Teach me to be a bridge builder in my relationships and show me how to reflect Your grace and kindness in my interactions with others. Strengthen me to love even those who are difficult to love, knowing that You love them too. I ask for Your presence to guide me in all my relationships, so that they may be a reflection of Your heart. In Jesus' name, Amen.

Reflection Questions:

1. How can you invite Jesus to be the center of your relationships?
2. What steps can you take to build or restore relationships that have been broken?
3. How can you reflect God's love to someone in your life who may be difficult to love?

Scripture for Meditation:

- "For there is one God and one mediator between God and mankind, the man Christ Jesus." — 1 Timothy 2:5
- "My old self has been crucified with Christ. It is no longer I who live, but Christ lives in me." — Galatians 2:20
- "Love one another as I have loved you." — John 15:12

Week 36: Hearing God's Voice

We are surrounded by countless voices every day. Some are voices of truth and love, while others are filled with lies, judgment, and negativity. These voices can sometimes wound us, making us feel small and insignificant. But amidst the noise, there is one voice that speaks life and love—a voice that never stops reminding us that we are deeply loved for all eternity. This is the voice of God, the Eternal One.

God's voice is the voice of love that comforts and reassures. When Jesus was baptized and began His ministry, the Father spoke from heaven and said, "This is my beloved Son, in whom I am well pleased" (Matthew 3:17). God doesn't speak often in the scriptures, but when He does, His words carry deep meaning. The message of love He spoke over Jesus is also true for us. In John 3:16-17, we are reminded that God sent His Son not to condemn the world but to save it. God's voice is not one of condemnation but of grace and acceptance.

To be called the Beloved of God is a profound reality. In a world filled with voices of condemnation, arrogance, and rejection, God's voice stands apart, reminding us that He loves us as we are. He sees our uniqueness, and rather than rejecting us, He embraces us with His love. The world's lies hold no power over us unless we choose to believe them. But we have a better option—to listen to God's truth. Jesus defeated evil, and He calls us to reject the lies of the enemy, whose only weapons are deception and fear (John 8:44).

Jesus showed us the radical nature of God's love. He didn't come to establish more religious rules or rituals. His message was different—He came to invite us into a relationship built on love and grace. Through Jesus, we can find true peace and wholeness in our relationships with God, others, and even with those who challenge us or cause us difficulty. Jesus' message was so powerful that the religious and political leaders of His time wanted to silence Him. They tried to stop His voice, but we know how that ended—His love triumphed over death and still speaks to us today.

To hear God's voice clearly, we must refuse the distractions of a performance-based, legalistic mindset. Instead, we need to become a community of faith that listens to God's voice and trusts in His love. When we allow the noise of the world to overwhelm us, we may begin to feel hopeless.

But when we listen to the still, small voice of God, calling us His Beloved, we find peace and assurance.

Dear friends, God is calling you His beloved son or daughter. This is your true identity. When we believe in God's perfect love, live in it, and proclaim it, we can cast out all fear. You are His, and nothing can separate you from His love.

Concluding Thought:

God's voice is the voice that matters most. It calls us His beloved, reminding us of who we are in Him. Let us turn down the noise of the world and tune our hearts to His voice of love and grace.

Closing Prayer:

Lord, thank You for calling me Your beloved. Help me to silence the lies of the world and listen only to Your voice. May I find comfort and peace in knowing that I am loved by You. Strengthen my heart to live out this truth and share it with others. Let Your perfect love cast out all my fears, and help me to trust in Your grace daily. In Jesus' name, Amen.

Reflection Questions:

1. What voices in your life are competing for your attention, and how can you focus more on hearing God's voice?
2. How does knowing that you are God's beloved change the way you see yourself and others?

3. What steps can you take to live out God's love and grace in your relationships with others?

Scripture for Meditation:

- "This is my beloved Son, in whom I am well pleased." — Matthew 3:17
- "My sheep hear my voice, and I know them, and they follow me." — John 10:27
- "There is no fear in love. But perfect love drives out fear..." — 1 John 4:18

Week 37: Putting Away All Prejudice

There has been much discussion about immigrants lately, and unfortunately, some of the comments have been negative. I remember my first visit to the USA in 1978 to attend a Youth Leadership conference for the church I was part of. Later, in 1980, I returned on a student visa to study theology and graduated in 1984. It wasn't until 1996 that my family and I moved to the USA as immigrants, where I began serving as a full-time pastor.

The truth is, no matter what negative things people may say about immigrants, the United States itself was built by immigrants. People came here from Europe, Africa, Asia, South America, and beyond. Historians even tell us that Native Americans were originally immigrants from Asia who traveled through the Bering land bridge many years ago. Despite this, I still remember that during my first month here, someone told me I didn't belong and that I should return to the Philippines. While it was painful to hear, I managed to smile, knowing that this person's ancestors had also come from another country. I could have easily said the same to him.

The journey of an immigrant is filled with challenges and uncertainty, and often, there's a sense of not quite belonging. They leave behind their homes, familiar faces, and everything they've ever known. They embark on a path of difficulties, navigating through a new culture, language, and way of life, all while holding on to the hope of finding a place to call home.

Interestingly, the Bible tells us that we are all immigrants. As Christians, we are also on a similar journey. Hebrews 11:13 describes us as "foreigners and strangers on earth." This world is not our permanent home. Our true citizenship is in heaven. Just like immigrants, we are passing through, learning how to navigate this life while keeping our eyes on our heavenly home.

Immigrants experience struggles that mirror our Christian walk. They leave behind everything familiar, just as we Christians long for our heavenly home where we will be reunited with God. They must learn new customs, languages, and ways of life, and often face misunderstandings and prejudice. Similarly, we must navigate a world whose values may conflict with our faith. Jesus said we are to be in the world but not of it (John 17:14-16).

As immigrants may struggle with identity, feeling torn between two worlds, so do Christians. We might be seen as outsiders for our faith, just as immigrants can be labeled because of their skin tone or accent. But our true identity is in Christ. We are children of God (1 John 3:1), and that is where our belonging lies, even when we feel out of place in this world. What truly matters is what God thinks of us, not the judgment of others.

The truth is, that we share more similarities than differences. Hebrews 11 reminds us that the heroes of faith were "looking forward to a better country—a heavenly one." They lived by faith, trusting God's promises, even when they did not see them fulfilled in their lifetime. Their faith was not in what this world could offer, but in the assurance of what God had prepared for them.

Why am I sharing this? Because just as immigrants hold on to the hope of a better life, we hold on to the hope of eternal life with Christ. It's this hope that sustains us through our trials and challenges. We are called to represent Christ in this world, to share His love, grace, and truth with those around us (2 Corinthians 5:20). Our lives should reflect the values of our heavenly home.

Yes, we are all immigrants in one way or another. We are all on a journey, looking forward to the promise of our Heavenly Father—a better country, a heavenly home where we will dwell with Him forever.

Concluding Thought:

As immigrants on earth and citizens of heaven, we are called to live with hope, representing Christ in all that we do. Let us remember that we are not alone in our journey, and our true home awaits us in God's presence.

Closing Prayer:

Dear Lord, thank You for reminding us that this world is not our final destination. Help us to live with hope, trusting in Your promises. Guide us as we navigate this life, and may we always reflect Your love and grace to others. Teach us to see every person, regardless of their background, as valuable in Your sight. Strengthen us as we look forward to our heavenly home. In Jesus' name, Amen.

Reflection Questions:

1. How does understanding your identity as a citizen of heaven impact how you live on earth?
2. Have you ever felt like an outsider, and how did you respond to those feelings?
3. How can you show Christ's love to immigrants or others who may feel out of place in this world?

Scripture for Meditation:

- "All these people were still living by faith when they died. They did not receive the things promised; they only saw them and welcomed them from a distance, admitting that they were foreigners and strangers on earth." — Hebrews 11:13 (NIV)

- "Our citizenship is in heaven, and we eagerly await a Savior from there, the Lord Jesus Christ." — Philippians 3:20 (NIV)
- "We are therefore Christ's ambassadors, as though God were making His appeal through us." — 2 Corinthians 5:20 (NIV)

Week 38: When The Unexpected Happens

It was one of the scariest moments in our lives. My wife and I were having our Thanksgiving celebration in the Los Angeles congregation I was serving as pastor at the time. However, my wife had to leave earlier because, as a wound treatment nurse, she needed to visit patients.

As she was walking down the street towards the parking lot at the back of the church facility, two young men began following her. When she entered the parking lot and was about to open her car, one of the men pulled a gun and pointed it at her, demanding that she give them her car keys.

It was a carjacking, but the terror of having a gun pointed at her was what truly shook her. At that moment, she thought it might be her last. She feared for her life, imagining the worst—being shot or seriously wounded. As a nurse, she knows well that bullet wounds cause severe damage and are extremely difficult to treat.

After the two men left with the car, my wife was in shock, trembling inside. In the days that followed, she experienced PTSD, and her blood pressure skyrocketed, landing her in the hospital.

One never knows what can happen in life. We like to think we're in control, but sudden and unexpected events can shatter that illusion. Whether it's a traumatic encounter, a sudden illness, or the loss of a loved one, life is unpredictable, and challenges can arise without warning.

Life is often a journey of twists and turns, filled with moments of joy and periods of struggle. Some challenges give us time to prepare, but others strike without notice, leaving us reeling in their wake. Unexpected illnesses, accidents, cancer diagnoses, or job losses can shatter our sense of normalcy and plunge us into a sea of uncertainty. During such moments, it's natural to feel overwhelmed, frightened, and even angry. Yet, God's Word provides us with a steadfast anchor for our souls.

These trials remind us of the fragility of life and the unpredictability of our earthly journey. They confront us with the reality that, despite our best efforts, control is often beyond our reach. Yet, these moments also present us with an opportunity to deepen our reliance on God and experience His presence in profound ways. My wife was praying silently throughout her experience, and it gave her the strength she needed in that frightening situation.

Sudden hardships can lead us to ask, "Why is this happening?" I've asked those questions myself. But scripture reassures us that God is near, even in our suffering. Psalm 34:18 tells us, "The Lord is close to the brokenhearted and saves those who are crushed in spirit." God is not a distant observer but a compassionate Savior who draws near to comfort and uphold us.

Trusting in God's sovereignty means believing that He can bring good out of even the most painful situations. It's difficult to grasp at times, but we have a God who promises to be with us always, even in the most challenging moments.

Romans 8:28 reminds us that "in all things, God works for the good of those who love Him, who have been called according to His purpose." This hope is not a denial of our pain but a confident assurance that God is at work, even in our darkest hours, bringing about His good purposes.

Concluding Thought:

Life may be unpredictable, but God is unchanging. In every trial and challenge, we can rest in His unwavering presence and trust that He is working for our good. He is our source of hope and strength, even when life feels out of control.

Closing Prayer:

Dear Lord, we thank You for Your constant presence in our lives, even when we face unexpected challenges and fears. Help us to trust You in every situation, knowing that You are working for our good. Give us the strength and courage to face whatever comes our way and remind us that Your love never fails. Comfort those who are brokenhearted and draw near to those who need You most. In Jesus' name, Amen.

Reflection Questions:

1. Can you think of a time when an unexpected hardship shook your sense of control? How did you respond?
2. How does trusting in God's sovereignty bring comfort during life's unpredictable moments?
3. How can you deepen your reliance on God when faced with sudden challenges?

Scripture for Meditation:

- "The Lord is close to the brokenhearted and saves those who are crushed in spirit." — Psalm 34:18 (NIV)
- "And we know that in all things God works for the good of those who love Him, who have been called according to His purpose." — Romans 8:28 (NIV)
- "Do not be anxious about anything, but in every situation, by prayer and petition, with thanksgiving, present your requests to God." — Philippians 4.6 (NIV)

Week 39: Lessons From Glaciers

My wife and I recently had the most amazing Alaskan cruise adventure. The highlight of the trip was passing through Glacier Bay. The cruise ship slowed down, allowing us to fully immerse ourselves in the majestic beauty of creation.

For this journey, we had a room with a balcony, and we spent our time either standing there or sitting on chairs, enjoying the view with our daughter, Carmel, and our two grandkids, Mia and Urijah.

I learned a little about glaciers during this trip, and they amazed me with their quiet power and patience. Glaciers are formed by the slow accumulation of snow over centuries, even millennia. Each glacier begins with a single snowflake, just like our faith begins with a simple act of belief. While a snowflake may seem insignificant on its own, over time, as more snow falls and compacts, it transforms into ice, becoming a powerful glacier.

Glaciers move at a slow pace—so slow, in fact, that their progress often goes unnoticed. Yet, despite this, glaciers carve valleys, shape mountains, and create fjords and inlets, like those we saw in Glacier Bay.

In our spiritual lives, growth often feels just as slow, and we may not see immediate results. However, just like the glaciers, the slow, steady work of the Holy Spirit within us is constantly molding us into the image of Christ. The Spirit is preparing us for the purposes God has for us, even when we don't see or feel it.

Looking at photos of the glaciers from years ago, I noticed that they haven't changed much. Patience is essential in the process of transformation. Just as glaciers slowly grow over time, our spiritual journey requires patience. James 1:4 reminds us to "let patience have its perfect work, that you may be perfect and complete, lacking nothing." Trusting in God's timing is crucial. We must surrender our desire for instant results and allow Him to work in His perfect way and time.

Another equally amazing lesson I observed is that glaciers often form in remote, quiet places. Our most significant spiritual growth also often occurs in the quiet, solitary moments spent with Jesus. In times of prayer, meditation, and reflection, we are transformed, just as the seemingly still glacier is constantly moving and changing beneath the surface.

Finally, glaciers endure. They withstand harsh conditions and pressure but continue moving forward. In the same way, as believers, we face trials and tribulations, but through them, we grow stronger. The Apostle Paul writes in Romans 5:3-4, "We glory in tribulations also: knowing that tribulation worketh patience; And patience, experience; and experience, hope."

May we embrace the slow, steady work of God in our lives, trusting that He is shaping us into something beautiful and powerful. Let us be patient, resilient, and steadfast, knowing that our faith, like a glacier, is gradually transforming the landscape of our hearts.

Concluding Thought:

Like glaciers, our spiritual journey may seem slow at times, but God is at work. Trust in His process, be patient, and remember that every small step forward brings transformation. God's work in us is both mighty and beautiful, even when we can't see it immediately.

Closing Prayer:

Dear Heavenly Father, thank You for patiently working in our lives. Help us trust in Your timing and surrender our desire for quick results. Mold us into the image of Your Son, Jesus Christ, and help us embrace the quiet, still moments where You do Your greatest work. May we endure through trials, knowing You are shaping us into something beautiful for Your purposes. In Jesus' name, Amen.

Reflection Questions:

1. In what areas of your life do you feel impatient about spiritual growth?
2. How can you embrace moments of stillness and solitude with God to grow in your faith?
3. What trials are you currently facing, and how is God using them to shape you?

Scripture for Meditation:

- James 1:4 (NIV) — "Let perseverance finish its work so that you may be mature and complete, not lacking anything."
- Romans 5:3-4 (NIV) — "Not only so, but we also glory in our sufferings, because we know that suffering produces perseverance; perseverance, character; and character, hope."
- Psalm 46:10 (NIV) — "Be still, and know that I am God."

Week 40: When God Is Silent

Not very many people know that there was a time in my life when I lost my voice for almost three months. No matter how hard I tried, no sound came out of my mouth. This happened in January 1989.

As a pastor, you can imagine how crucial my voice was to my ministry. Through preaching, teaching, mentoring, and comforting, I served. During the first month of having no voice, I struggled deeply. People would ask me questions, and I had to write my responses on a pad of paper—there was no texting back then! It tested my patience and became a profound journey of learning what it means to wait on the Lord.

What made it even worse was when a doctor, after examining my throat, told me that I might have cancer. A second opinion from another doctor confirmed the same suspicion, which left me terrified. However, a third doctor said that I would get better. I chose to believe the third doctor!

Yet, by the second month, I still had no voice. Frustrated, I wrote a letter to my supervisor offering my resignation, explaining that I could not fulfill my duties as a pastor without a voice. He responded with encouragement and simply said, "Be patient and wait on the Lord."

By the third month, my feelings of helplessness grew. I questioned how I could fulfill my calling if I couldn't speak. But it was in this silence that God began to teach me invaluable lessons about His power and my dependence on Him. I realized that my voice, while important, was not the only way God could work through me.

During those quiet months, I found new ways to connect with my church family. I listened more intently, prayed more deeply, and discovered God's presence in the stillness. Interestingly, my inability to speak became an opportunity to hear God's voice more clearly. Sometimes, silence is God's answer, but it never means He has abandoned us. In His silence, I learned to wait and trust in His love.

Isaiah 40:31 reminds us that those who wait on the Lord will renew their strength. During my silence, God renewed me in unexpected ways—providing physical rest, spiritual rejuvenation, and emotional healing. My strength didn't come from my ability to speak but from God's sustaining grace.

Without my voice, I had to rely on other forms of communication. This opened my eyes to the various ways God speaks to us—through His Word, through the quiet whisper of the Holy Spirit, and through the actions and words of others. Additionally, my inability to speak allowed others to step up and take leadership roles, including one man who would go on to become the National Director in the Philippines and Superintendent of Missions in Asia.

Waiting on the Lord requires faith and patience. This period of silence tested my trust in God's timing and plan. I had to surrender my need for control and lean into His promise that He is always working for our good, even when we cannot see it. Three months later, during the Holy Week season, my voice finally returned.

If you are in a season of waiting or silence, remember that God is with you. He is faithful. He is renewing your strength, teaching you new things, and deepening your faith. Trust in His timing and embrace the quiet moments, for it is often in the silence that we hear His voice most clearly.

Concluding Thought:

Even in the silence, God is working. When we feel lost, helpless, or unsure, we can trust that He is moving in ways we cannot see. Be encouraged—His silence is not an absence but an invitation to deepen our dependence on Him.

Closing Prayer:

Heavenly Father, thank You for the lessons You teach us in the quiet seasons of our lives. Help us to trust Your timing and rely on Your strength. In moments when we feel helpless or frustrated, remind us that You are with us, renewing our spirits and guiding us. Thank You for Your faithful love and for speaking to us, even in the silence. In Jesus' name, Amen.

Reflection Questions:

1. Have you ever experienced a season of silence in your life where it seemed like God was quiet? How did you respond?
2. What is something you can do to deepen your trust in God during times of waiting?
3. How can silence be a tool for growth in your relationship with God?

Scripture for Meditation:

- Isaiah 40:31 (NIV) — "But those who hope in the Lord will renew their strength. They will soar on wings like eagles; they will run and not grow weary, they will walk and not be faint."
- Psalm 46:10 (NIV) — "Be still, and know that I am God."
- Romans 8:28 (NIV) — "And we know that in all things God works for the good of those who love him, who have been called according to his purpose."

Week 41: The Wind and Waves Obey

We had a great discussion yesterday at church facilitated by our pastor about the story of Jesus calming the storm, found in Mark 4:35-41.

After finishing preaching to a crowd, Jesus boarded a boat with His disciples following Him. He must have been very tired after a long day.

As they crossed the Sea of Galilee, a massive storm arose, and water began filling their boat. Yet, Jesus was asleep! Despite having witnessed many miracles performed by Jesus, the disciples panicked and feared for their safety because He was sleeping.

In their panic, they urgently woke Jesus, expressing their danger. Jesus then rebuked the wind and waves, and even the disciples, saying, "Where is your faith?" They were afraid and amazed, wondering, "Who is this? Even the wind and the waves obey Him!"

This story resonates with me personally. When I was in the Philippines, twice I was in boats that were nearly capsized by waves, and in other situations, three times I nearly drowned, but was saved by others. Reading this story, I empathize with the disciples' panic. It's striking to contrast Jesus' calm amidst the storm with the disciples' turmoil. At that moment, their fear of the storm outweighed their trust in God.

For me, this story highlights essential truths about our journey with Christ. In our humanity, we often focus only on the present moment. The disciples reacted much like we would have, seeing only the looming threat of the waves. Many of Jesus' disciples were fishermen and had faced storms before, but this one so terrified them that they feared for their lives.

During the storm, the disciples should have remembered the miracles they had seen with Jesus, yet they panicked instead of trusting Him. Jesus had already told them they would reach the other side, but in their fear, they forgot His words and His character.

We can all relate to the disciples in such moments. It's easier to trust God when times are good, but in difficult times, trusting Him becomes more crucial.

Life is unpredictable; storms will come, but God's unchanging character provides a steady foundation when everything feels uncertain. As Christians, Jesus lives within us through the Holy Spirit, always present with us.

He's got this! Let's never forget that. Instead, let's pray to Jesus: "This situation is uncomfortable and stressful, but I trust You, my Lord! Give me strength, guide me through this trial, and teach me what You will. Thank You for Your love and protection, even in troubled times." Let's trust in Jesus and let the Holy Spirit calm us.

Concluding Thought:

Life's storms are inevitable, but Jesus is always present, ready to calm both the external and internal turmoil. We can trust Him, even when the waves feel overwhelming, knowing He is greater than the storm.

Closing Prayer:

Heavenly Father, thank You for being with us through every storm. Help us to trust You, even when fear overwhelms us. Calm the storms in our hearts, remind us of Your love, and teach us to rely on You completely. Strengthen our faith and let us rest in the assurance that You are always in control. In Jesus' name, Amen.

Reflection Questions:

1. When have you felt overwhelmed by life's storms, and how did you respond?

2. How can you remind yourself to trust Jesus during difficult situations?
3. What can you do to strengthen your faith so that you can rely on God's promises in challenging times?

Scripture for Meditation:

- Mark 4:39-40 (NIV) — "He got up, rebuked the wind and said to the waves, 'Quiet! Be still!' Then the wind died down and it was completely calm. He said to his disciples, 'Why are you so afraid? Do you still have no faith?'"
- Isaiah 26:3 (NIV) — "You will keep in perfect peace those whose minds are steadfast because they trust in You."
- Psalm 46:1-3 (NIV) — "God is our refuge and strength, an ever-present help in trouble. Therefore we will not fear, though the earth give way and the mountains fall into the heart of the sea."

Week 42: Meandering in Our Journey

There's a common perception that a straight path is the only way forward, that if we aren't moving directly toward our goals, we must be lost. But life doesn't always follow a straight line. Sometimes, we find ourselves meandering—taking detours, exploring new paths, and pausing along the way. In these moments, it's easy to feel like we're off course, like we've lost our way. But what if these meanderings are not signs of being lost, but rather opportunities to listen, meditate, and enjoy God's creation?

God, in Every Step

Now that I'm retired, I've found more time to take walks. When I walk, I intentionally decide not to have a fixed direction. One of my favorite places to visit is the Los Angeles Arboretum, a vast park in the heart of Los Angeles County. When I enter the park, I allow my feet to lead me wherever they will.

Meandering lets us move at a pace that allows us to notice things we might otherwise overlook. The vibrant colors of a sunset, the gentle rustling of leaves, or the Holy Spirit's quiet promptings are treasures often missed if we're too focused on getting from point A to point B. But when we meander, we slow down, breathe, and start to see the world through God's eyes. At the Arboretum, I've discovered plants and flowers I had never seen before. Each visit feels like a small adventure, and I love it!

Whenever I meander, I stop to examine my discoveries. I take the time to smell the flowers or even the leaves. In the Australian section of the Arboretum, there are dozens of eucalyptus trees, each with its own unique scent. Some smell like mint, others like medicine, and one even smells like asphalt. On one of my walks, I stumbled upon a tree nestled among others, bearing fruits I had never seen before. A sign beneath it identified it as a Rose Apple. Curious, I picked one and smelled it—it had the fragrance of a rose. After a quick search on Google, I found out it was edible, so I took a bite. It tasted like an apple, reminiscent of the Filipino "makopa." Such is the blessing of meandering; I discover new things all the time.

These walks are also a time for reflection, and as I ponder, I often discover new things within myself. Meditation during these moments brings inspiration and insight.

Consider the Israelites in the wilderness. Were they truly lost, or did God purposely cause them to meander? Is it possible that their journey to the Promised Land took forty years, not because they were lost, but because God was teaching them, shaping them, and revealing Himself to them? Their path was winding, filled with moments of doubt and faith, disobedience and grace. Yet through it all, God was with them, leading them even when the way seemed unclear.

In our own lives, meandering can be a time of deep spiritual growth. It's in the pauses and detours that we often hear God's voice most clearly. We learn to trust His timing, to find joy in the present moment, and to appreciate the beauty of the journey, not just the destination.

So, when you find yourself meandering, don't rush to get back on the "right" path. Instead, embrace the opportunity to listen to God, to meditate on His Word, and to enjoy the wonders of His creation. Remember that even when the path seems unclear, God is guiding your steps. You are not lost; you are exactly where He wants you to be.

Concluding Thought

Life's journey is not always a straight line, but it is always under the guidance of our loving God. Trust that every detour, every pause, and every meander is part of His perfect plan to draw you closer to Him and to reveal more of His presence in your life.

Closing Prayer

Heavenly Father, thank You for the unexpected paths and quiet moments that You lead us into. Help us to trust in Your timing and to find peace in the journey, even when it feels uncertain. May we learn to listen for Your voice in the stillness and to appreciate the beauty of Your creation as we walk with You. Guide our steps, Lord, and remind us that we are never truly lost, for You are always with us. In Jesus' name, Amen.

Reflection Questions

1. Have you experienced moments in life where you felt like you were meandering? How did God reveal Himself during those times?
2. What blessings or lessons have you discovered during seasons where the path was unclear?
3. How can you make time to slow down and enjoy God's presence in the ordinary moments of your day?

Scripture for Meditation

- "The heart of man plans his way, but the Lord establishes his steps." – Proverbs 16:9 (ESV)

Week 43: The Deep Things of God

A few years ago, my wife and I joined a tour group with my high school classmates from the USA to visit the Sumaguing Caves in the mountains of Sagada, Philippines. Although I couldn't participate in the adventure due to a mild flu, my wife's testimony speaks wonders about the cave.

Known as the Big Cave, Sumaguing is perhaps the most popular and frequently visited cave on the island of Luzon. It boasts the largest chamber of all the connecting caves in town (with over 60 known caves beneath Sagada). To see the magnificent formations of stalactites and stalagmites that took thousands, even millions, of years to shape, one must trek down a slippery trail. Nature has sculpted these formations into unique shapes with fanciful names like king and queen's curtains, Mickey Mouse, pregnant woman, and more. Inside, you find underground streams and pools of freezing cold water.

Deep things intrigue us—whether it's deep jungles, deep water, or even deep caves. But the greatest depths are found in the spiritual realm. God calls us to go deeper with Him. In 1 Corinthians 2:10, it says, "The Spirit searches all things, even the depths of God." He invites us not to be content with surface-level faith but to explore the richness of His wisdom and presence.

Romans 11:33 echoes this truth: "Oh, the depth of the riches both of the wisdom and knowledge of God! How unsearchable are His judgments and unfathomable His ways!" God's ways are beyond our understanding, yet He beckons us to draw nearer, to go deeper, and to seek intimacy with Him.

It's not enough to simply know about Jesus. He calls us into a deeper, more personal relationship. Revelation 3:20 says, "Here I am! I stand at the door and knock. If anyone hears my voice and opens the door, I will come in and eat with that person, and they with me." This invitation to dine with Jesus is a call to intimacy, a relationship that goes beyond mere acknowledgment of Him as Savior.

The Apostle Paul understood this. Even after all the miracles, letters, and hardships he faced, he still expressed a desire to know Christ more. In Philippians 3:10, he writes, "I want to know Christ—yes, to know the power of his resurrection…" Even with all Paul had done, his deepest longing was to know Jesus more intimately.

In the story of Mary and Martha, Jesus praised Mary for choosing to sit at His feet and listen (Luke 10:38-42). Martha was busy with many things, but Jesus said Mary had chosen what was better. In the same way, we are called to prioritize intimacy with Jesus, to sit at His feet and grow in our relationship with Him.

Richard Foster, in his book *Celebration of Discipline*, says, "Superficiality is the curse of our age. The doctrine of instant satisfaction is our primary spiritual problem." Our culture promotes instant gratification, but the depth of our relationship with God cannot be rushed. It takes time, dedication, and a longing for more of Him.

Thirsting for More of God Psalms 42:1-2 says, "As the deer pants for streams of water, so my soul pants for you, my God. My soul thirsts for God, for the living God." If we find ourselves tired of shallow spirituality, then it's time to dive deeper into our relationship with Jesus. Just as a deer longs for water, our souls should long for more of God. He offers us living water that satisfies, filling the deepest parts of our hearts.

Concluding Thought:

God invites us to go deeper, to seek more than just surface-level faith. Let's open the door to Jesus, allowing Him to enter and take us on a journey of intimacy, wisdom, and unsearchable depth.

Closing Prayer:

Heavenly Father, thank You for the invitation to go deeper with You. We long to know You more and to experience the fullness of Your love and presence. Help us to seek intimacy with You daily and to be open to the depths of Your wisdom. Teach us to trust in Your ways, even when we don't fully understand them. In Jesus' name, Amen.

Reflection Questions:

1. In what areas of your faith do you feel you are only at the surface level?
2. How can you take steps to deepen your relationship with God this week?
3. Are there any distractions in your life preventing you from going deeper with Jesus?

Scripture for Meditation:

- Psalms 42:1-2 — "As the deer pants for streams of water, so my soul pants for you, my God. My soul thirsts for God, for the living God."
- 1 Corinthians 2:10 — "The Spirit searches all things, even the depths of God."
- Romans 11:33 — "Oh, the depth of the riches of the wisdom and knowledge of God! How unsearchable his judgments, and his paths beyond tracing out!"

Week 44: Finding Joy Beyond Material Wealth

After our morning exercise, a group of us decided to have lunch at one of our favorite places. We love this spot not only for its delicious food at reasonable prices but yesterday, to our surprise, the prices jumped—Inflation! Many of us have noticed this increase almost everywhere around the world.

If you've recently purchased gas, groceries, or anything else, you've likely experienced some shock and stress, especially for those who don't have much. It can be distressing, but remember, you're not alone. Yet, worrying won't change the situation.

How we handle this stress largely depends on how we view money. If our happiness is tied to how much wealth or material comfort we have, we may find ourselves on shaky ground.

True Wealth: Relationships and Kindness

Scripture reminds us that true happiness isn't found in accumulating wealth but in the relationships, we nurture, the kindness we show, and the purpose we find in serving others. Moments of laughter, acts of generosity, and meaningful experiences are what truly enrich our lives.

1 Timothy 6:6-10 (The Message) puts it this way: "A devout life does bring wealth, but it's the rich simplicity of being yourself before God. Since we entered the world penniless and will leave it penniless, if we have bread on the table and shoes on our feet, that's enough. But if it's only money these leaders are after, they'll self-destruct in no time. Lust for money brings trouble and nothing but trouble. Going down that path, some lose their footing in the faith completely and live to regret it bitterly ever after."

The apostle Peter echoes this sentiment in 1 Peter 1:8-9. He talks about the kind of joy that comes not from material possessions but from our faith in Jesus. Though we haven't seen Him, our belief in Him fills us with an "inexpressible and glorious joy." This joy is beyond words and surpasses our understanding. It's a joy that isn't tied to wealth, but rather the assurance of our salvation and the presence of Jesus in our lives through the Holy Spirit.

Shifting Our Focus

Ultimately, the pursuit of happiness isn't about acquiring more wealth or possessions but about embracing love, compassion, and a meaningful purpose. True contentment comes from living in the present moment and cultivating a grateful heart, regardless of our financial situation.

Proverbs 17:22 reminds us: "A joyful heart is good medicine, but a crushed spirit dries up the bones."

Let us shift our focus from material wealth to inner wealth—the wealth of love, kindness, and gratitude. In the end, it's not the size of our bank account that determines our happiness, but the richness of our hearts.

Concluding Thought:

True joy is not found in worldly riches but in a life filled with love, faith, and service to others. Let's strive for a heart that overflows with compassion, kindness, and gratitude, trusting in God's provision for all our needs.

Closing Prayer:

Heavenly Father, thank You for reminding us where true joy is found. Help us not to be consumed by the pursuit of material things but to focus on nurturing relationships, showing kindness, and serving others. Fill our hearts with Your inexpressible joy and guide us to live a life of contentment and purpose. In Jesus' name, Amen.

Reflection Questions:

1. How do you currently view money and material wealth? Is it a source of joy or stress in your life?
2. In what ways can you shift your focus from material wealth to inner richness—such as kindness, compassion, and gratitude?
3. How can you serve others and experience the joy that comes from giving?

Scripture for Meditation:

- 1 Timothy 6:6-10 — "A devout life does bring wealth, but it's the rich simplicity of being yourself before God."
- 1 Peter 1:8-9 — "Though you have not seen him, you love him; and even though you do not see him now, you believe in him and are filled with an inexpressible and glorious joy."
- Proverbs 17:22 — "A joyful heart is good medicine, but a crushed spirit dries up the bones."

Week 45: Ordinary People Empowered

At church last week, our pastor asked how we would feel if we witnessed the Holy Spirit descending upon the apostles, enabling them to speak in a way that everyone in the crowd could understand in their own languages. That must have been an incredible experience—witnessing such a miracle! Can you imagine the gospel being proclaimed in different languages? I would be so thrilled if I heard them speak in my dialect, Kapampangan. And to think, they didn't even have Google Translate back then!

This miraculous event marked the birth of the Church and emphasized the universal mission of spreading the Good News to the whole world.

What I find particularly encouraging is how Pentecost underscores the empowerment of ordinary people. The disciples were not extraordinary by worldly standards. They were fishermen, tax collectors, and common folk with no special social or religious standing—just like any regular person. Yet, through the Holy Spirit, they were transformed into powerful witnesses of Christ's resurrection.

This reminds us that God often chooses the humble and the unassuming to accomplish His purposes. As Paul writes in 1 Corinthians 1:27-29: *"But God chose the foolish things of the world to shame the wise; God chose the weak things of the world to shame the strong."*

This is a powerful encouragement for all of us. It's empowering! No matter our background, education, or social status, the Holy Spirit can work through us. Our weaknesses and limitations do not disqualify us from being vessels of His power. In fact, they make space for God's strength to shine even brighter.

The Spirit of God not only empowered individuals but also formed them into a new kind of community. The early believers were drawn together into a fellowship marked by unity, generosity, and mutual support. Acts 2:44-47 describes how they shared everything in common, met regularly for worship, and broke bread together with glad and sincere hearts.

In today's divided world, this model of a Spirit-filled community is more relevant than ever. It challenges us to move beyond individualism and embrace a lifestyle of interdependence and communal care. As Christians, we are called to create and nurture communities where love, generosity, and genuine fellowship are visible expressions of our faith. Pentecost reminds us that we are not alone; we are part of the body of Christ, connected by the Holy Spirit.

The congregation I am with is small. We may seem insignificant, but the Spirit that works within us is strong. The descent of the Spirit was not a one-time event but the beginning of an ongoing process of sanctification and empowerment. In Ephesians 5:18, we are encouraged to "be filled with the Spirit," implying a continuous action rather than a one-time occurrence.

For us today, this means that our spiritual journey is dynamic and progressive. The Holy Spirit is constantly at work within us—convicting, guiding, comforting, and equipping us for service. We are invited to remain open and responsive to His leading, allowing Him to mold us more into the likeness of Christ.

Concluding Thought:

The same Spirit that empowered the apostles at Pentecost is at work in us today. We may be ordinary people, but through the Holy Spirit, we are given extraordinary power to live out our faith and share God's love with the world.

Closing Prayer:

Heavenly Father, thank You for the gift of the Holy Spirit who empowers and guides us every day. Help us to be open to His leading, to trust in Your strength even in our weakness, and to embrace our calling as part of the body of Christ. Fill us with Your Spirit, so that we may reflect Your love and grace in all that we do. In Jesus' name, Amen.

Reflection Questions:

1. How can you remain open and responsive to the Holy Spirit's leading in your life?
2. What areas of your life do you feel weak or unqualified, and how can you trust the Holy Spirit to work through those areas?
3. How can you help foster a Spirit-filled community marked by unity and generosity in your local church or fellowship?

Scripture for Meditation:

- Acts 2:44-47 — "All the believers were together and had everything in common. They sold property and possessions to give to anyone who had need. Every day they continued to meet together in the temple courts. They broke bread in their homes and ate together with glad and sincere hearts, praising God and enjoying the favor of all the people."
- 1 Corinthians 1:27-29 — "But God chose the foolish things of the world to shame the wise; God chose the weak things of the world to shame the strong."
- Ephesians 5:18 — "Do not get drunk on wine, which leads to debauchery. Instead, be filled with the Spirit."

Week 46: Finding God In The Storm

Earlier this year, I went on an exciting trip with my brother, Ferdie, to the beautiful paradise of El Nido, Palawan. This place is famous for its breathtaking beauty and amazing island-hopping adventures. We were thrilled to explore every part of it. We had two days of island-hopping fun planned, each promising new and exciting experiences.

On the second day, we started our journey early, heading to the farthest island on a motorized boat with twenty other eager tourists. The trip began smoothly, with the sun shining brightly and the sea sparkling like diamonds. But then, the wind started blowing. It wasn't just any wind but a fierce, strong gust that turned our peaceful adventure into a wild and suspenseful journey.

The one-hour trip took much longer as our boat struggled through the rough waters. The calm sea transformed into a roaring monster, with waves crashing against the boat and soaking everyone on board. Each huge wave lifted the boat high into the air before dropping it with a heavy thud, making us feel like we might capsize at any moment.

It was a scary experience, filled with moments of fear. The beautiful scenery around us, now covered in mist and sea spray, made everything even more dramatic. Every passenger clung tightly to their seats and life jackets, whispering prayers in their hearts.

As I think back on that day, the memory is vivid— showing the raw power of the sea that drew me closer to God. I found myself praying, "God save us!" and now, looking back, I smile at the experience—but I wasn't smiling then! (smile)

A Storm in the Life of Paul

The apostle Paul experienced something even more terrifying. In Acts 27:14-15, a fierce wind called the "northeaster" rushed down upon the ship he was on. The wind was so strong that the ship was caught in it and was driven uncontrollably for days. The crew made desperate attempts to stay afloat, but eventually, they ran aground near the island of Malta. The ship was wrecked, and everyone had to swim ashore on pieces of the broken vessel.

Malta wasn't their intended destination, but it's where they ended up. Storms can do that—wash you ashore in unfamiliar places, among unfamiliar people. However, Paul soon discovered that Malta was full of opportunities. The islanders welcomed them, and Paul found that God had sent him there for a reason. The father of the island's leading man was sick, and Paul prayed for him, resulting in his healing. After that, many other sick people came to Paul and were healed (Acts 28:7-9).

If it hadn't been for the storm, Paul wouldn't have ended up on Malta. God's plans weren't hindered by the storm. Instead, He used it to lead Paul to a place where amazing things could happen.

Finding Purpose in the Storm

Think about the people of Malta—they may have been praying for help, wondering if anyone would come. Little did they know that their answer would arrive in the form of a storm. While Paul was praying on the sea, trusting that God would lead him to his destination, God was steering him to be the answer to someone else's prayers.

Are you in a storm right now? Are you aware of the unexpected places it's taking you and the new people it's introducing you to? When you're feeling frustrated or confused about where life's latest storm has taken you, remember that God is using the storm to connect your life with His purpose. The storm may be the tool God uses to answer your prayers while also using you to bless others.

Concluding Thought:

Storms in life can seem frightening and chaotic, but they never shipwreck God's plans for us. He uses even the most turbulent times to lead us to places of purpose, where we can bless others and be blessed ourselves.

Closing Prayer:

Heavenly Father, thank You for Your guidance and presence in the storms of life. Help us to trust You, even when we can't see the way forward. Teach us to embrace the storms, knowing that You are working in and through them for our good and for the good of others. May we find strength in You and be open to the new opportunities You bring us through life's challenges. In Jesus' name, Amen.

Reflection Questions:

1. Can you recall a time when a difficult situation in your life led to unexpected blessings or new opportunities?
2. How can you trust God more in the midst of your current struggles, knowing that He is in control?
3. How might God be using you to answer someone else's prayers during your own storm?

Scripture for Meditation:

- Acts 27:14-15 — "A fierce wind called the "northeaster" rushed down from the island. Since the ship was caught and unable to head into the wind, we gave way to it and were driven along."

- Romans 8:28 — "And we know that in all things God works for the good of those who love him, who have been called according to his purpose."
- Psalm 107:28-29 — "Then they cried to the Lord in their trouble, and he brought them out of their distress. He stilled the storm to a whisper; the waves of the sea were hushed."

Week 47: A Love Story

One aspect of my life I will always remember is when I first met my wife at a church youth conference. I felt something strange—my heart palpitated when I first saw her, and that feeling only grew stronger as we continued to see each other at the seminary where we both became students. Can you relate? It's like your heart dances whenever you're with that special someone.

It was like an empty void I never knew existed suddenly got filled. It was an amazing journey with her. I guess that's what they call being in love. Flowers, beaches, mountains, stars, and this lady, Carmelita—all intertwined in the realm of beauty.

Truly, winning the lottery pales in comparison. Being near her was like witnessing the Independence Day fireworks. How do I describe it? It felt like being in a sanctuary filled with warmth and acceptance, a place where love and comfort were always present when we went on dates.

This May 20th will be our 40th wedding anniversary. How fast time flew! Through the years, I've learned that love also means trust and commitment to one another. It means being willing to give my all for her, sharing her laughter, and sometimes, shedding tears when she cried.

If you've experienced love, you probably understand what I'm saying, right? But now, there is another kind of love that's even more powerful. Have you ever considered your relationship with Jesus as something like "falling in love"? Some might find this comparison unconventional when thinking about our connection with God. Yet, the Apostle Paul likened our relationship with God to an intimate love relationship, illustrating it in the metaphor of a bride and groom (Ephesians 5:25, 32).

Did you know that there is an entire book in the Bible that is deeply romantic? It's the Song of Songs. It's not solely a romantic poem for spouses but an invitation for all of us to deepen our intimacy with Jesus, our spiritual Bridegroom.

In this sacred text, Jesus is portrayed as the bridegroom, His Spirit depicted as one who leaps across mountains and soars over hills to draw close to us. He stands intimately before us, singing a love song: "Arise, my precious one, my lovely one, and come with me. See, the winter is past; the rains are over and gone. Flowers appear on the earth; the season of singing has come" (Song of Songs 2:8-12).

Jesus' time on earth was filled with challenges. In His culture, the religious elite displayed arrogance, legalism, and elitism, condemning those who didn't conform to their traditions. Yet in a troubled society full of hypocrites and sinners, how was Jesus able to love others so deeply?

He could have sought worldly success, proven His teachings superior to the greatest thinkers, or become a political leader. But Jesus chose differently. His greatest joy was loving God and sharing that love with others (Mark 12:30-31). His love came from an intimacy with the Father, and His life's rhythm harmonized with God's Spirit.

Jesus exemplified love, teaching us that the kingdom of heaven is like a merchant who sells everything to buy a precious pearl (Matthew 13:45). He gave up everything—even His life—to show His love, to reconcile us to God, and to make us His own.

This love story compels us to return His love and extend it to others. One day, there will be a great Wedding Feast in heaven, where Jesus, the bridegroom, will gather His beloved. You and I are invited, for we are His beloved.

Concluding Thought:

The love between a husband and wife is a beautiful reflection of the greater love that Christ has for His Church.

As we experience love in our relationships, let us also deepen our love and intimacy with Jesus, our heavenly Bridegroom.

Closing Prayer:

Lord Jesus, thank You for the deep and unfailing love You have for us. Help us to understand and receive that love, and guide us to share it with others. May we grow in intimacy with You and reflect Your love in all our relationships. Amen.

Reflection Questions:

1. Can you recall a moment when you felt God's love in a powerful way?
2. How does thinking about your relationship with Jesus as a love story impact the way you connect with Him?
3. In what ways can you show Christlike love to the people in your life?

Scripture for Meditation:

- Ephesians 5:25 — "Husbands, love your wives, just as Christ loved the church and gave himself up for her."
- Song of Songs 2:8-12 — "Arise, my precious one, my lovely one, and come with me. See, the winter is past; the rains are over and gone. Flowers appear on the earth; the season of singing has come."
- Matthew 13:45-46 — "Again, the kingdom of heaven is like a merchant looking for fine pearls. When he found one of great value, he went away and sold everything he had and bought it."

Week 48: The Cry of a Broken Heart

When I first read the story of Job's wife telling him to "curse God and die" (Job 2:9), I was shocked. My initial reaction was, "How could she say such a thing? How disrespectful to God!"

But over time, I began to understand that her words came from a place of deep, overwhelming despair. Imagine the grief she carried—losing not only their property but, most tragically, all their children. On top of that, she had to watch her husband sitting on a heap of ashes, covered in painful boils.

Who wouldn't feel heartbroken, angry, and confused? If I were in her position, I might have reacted the same way.

When we look at her situation through the lens of compassion, we can see that she was enduring unbearable grief. Her words, though harsh, reflected a heart filled with hopelessness. She wasn't just angry at their circumstances; she may have also felt betrayed by God, whom they had served so faithfully. Seeing Job in such physical and emotional agony likely deepened her pain, making death seem preferable to a life so full of suffering.

Did she really mean it? Her words might not have revealed her true belief about God but rather her shattered emotions in that moment. Haven't we all said things we didn't mean when we were hurting? Sometimes, intense suffering clouds our judgment, and we say things out of pain that we would never say otherwise. Job's wife was likely grappling with the impossible task of reconciling her faith with the weight of her losses. Her words were the cry of a heart in agony, not the final verdict of her faith.

Yet God, in His infinite mercy, understood her pain. He sees beyond our words and actions to the broken hearts beneath them. While her statement may have seemed unfaithful, God's response was not condemnation but patience. He knows the depths of human suffering and the weakness of our hearts in times of crisis. As Psalm 34:18 reminds us, "The Lord is close to the brokenhearted and saves those who are crushed in spirit."

The story of Job and his wife points us to a God who is merciful and compassionate, even when we falter. Her reaction, though flawed, reflects the raw reality of grief that can test our faith. But God, who understands the struggles we face, remains faithful. He is there in our lowest moments, ready to extend His grace, mercy, and forgiveness.

In times of despair, we can be comforted knowing that our loving Father sees beyond our outbursts of pain and offers healing and hope. No matter how dark our situation may feel, His understanding heart is always ready to welcome us back into His embrace.

Concluding Thought:

When we are in the deepest valleys of pain and grief, it's easy to say things we don't mean. But God sees through our pain and knows our hearts. Even in our most broken moments, He remains near, offering His healing and compassion.

Closing Prayer:

Heavenly Father, thank You for Your compassion, even in our moments of weakness and despair. Forgive us when our words are filled with pain rather than faith. Please heal our hearts, restore our hope, and remind us that You are always near, ready to carry us through our suffering. In Jesus' name, Amen.

Reflection Questions:

1. Can you recall a time when you said something out of pain or despair that you didn't truly mean?

2. How can you remind yourself of God's nearness when life feels overwhelming?
3. In what ways can you extend compassion to others who are grieving or hurting?

Scripture for Meditation:

- Psalm 34:18 — "The Lord is close to the brokenhearted and saves those who are crushed in spirit."
- Matthew 11:28 — "Come to me, all you who are weary and burdened, and I will give you rest."

Week 49: The Plans We Make

Reflecting on my journey recently, I've realized just how different my path has been from my initial hopes. Did I ever anticipate or desire to become a pastor? Not really. Back in high school, my passions leaned more toward science and math, with history and literature coming in third and fourth. I dreamed of becoming a scientist or an engineer. To make a long story short, it didn't happen.

I have close friends who wondered why I "wasted" my time and foolishly chose a different path. Honestly, there were moments when I thought the same. Many of us harbor ambitions and dreams, longing to steer our destinies and fulfill our aspirations. But in my case, I learned that God had a different path laid out.

Perhaps some of you can relate. You make plans only to find that God has something entirely different in mind. Yes, I'm talking about living life on God's terms—not my terms.

When I reflect on the stories of Jesus in the scriptures, I see Him entering people's lives on His terms. He surprises them, intervenes unexpectedly, and changes their lives in ways they never imagined. Jesus deliberately crossed paths with the Samaritan woman, altering her life's course according to His plan, not hers (John 4:4-42).

Similarly, Paul encountered Jesus on the road to Damascus, and his life transformed according to Christ's terms, not his own (Acts 9). The same pattern emerges with Noah, Abraham, Moses, David, Esther, and countless others—all learning to submit to God's plans.

This intervention isn't confined to biblical figures; it extends to us as well. God's love is so profound that when He sees us veering away from His way of life and truth, He intervenes to offer us a new life. A detour may not be a detour after all. It may be the real path for us.

Choosing to live life on Jesus' terms means placing Him at the forefront of our journey. Jesus calls us to deny ourselves and carry our cross, not to burden us, but because He knows that true fulfillment lies in wholeheartedly following Him. In yielding to Jesus, we discover that amidst life's turmoil, His peace becomes our anchor; in adversity, His strength sustains us; and within uncertainty, His hope toughens our souls.

What are your plans? Are you living life according to your terms, or are you open to the possibility that God may have something different in mind for you? Perhaps He wants you to walk His path, even when it seems like a detour from your own.

As we navigate this journey, let's remember the words of Jeremiah 29:11, "For I know the plans I have for you," declares the Lord, "plans to prosper you and not to harm you, plans to give you hope and a future." We may not fully understand God's plans, but one thing I've learned—His plans are always the best.

Concluding Thought:

God's path for us may not align with our personal ambitions, but His plans are always better, leading us to a life of fulfillment and purpose in Him. Trust His direction, even when it takes unexpected turns.

Closing Prayer:

Heavenly Father, help us surrender our plans and dreams to You. Teach us to trust Your perfect will for our lives. Lead us, Lord, to live on Your terms and not our own, so that we may experience the fullness of Your peace, love, and purpose. In Jesus' name, Amen.

Reflection Questions:

1. Have you experienced moments when your plans didn't align with God's, and how did you respond?
2. How can you practice trusting God with your future, even when it seems uncertain?
3. What steps can you take to surrender your own ambitions and seek God's direction for your life?

Scripture for Meditation:

- Jeremiah 29:11 — "For I know the plans I have for you," declares the Lord, "plans to prosper you and not to harm you, plans to give you hope and a future."
- John 4:4-42 — Jesus' encounter with the Samaritan woman, showing how He redirects our lives according to His purpose.
- Acts 9 — The conversion of Paul, revealing the transformative power of submitting to God's terms.

Week 50: Shaken To the Core

There are moments in our lives that shake us to our core. Some moments challenge our understanding of God's presence and care. For some, these moments come unexpectedly, like a sudden storm on a calm sea. For others, they linger like a persistent shadow, casting doubt on the very foundation of our beliefs. One such moment etched itself into my memory as a young boy in our small neighborhood in the Philippines. It is a memory that has altered my perception of God.

There was a group of children playing by a murky river close to where I grew up. You could hear their laughter mingling with the gentle flow of water. Among them was E…, an innocent young boy, carefree and unaware of the tragedy that awaited. In a heartbeat, joy turned to panic as E… disappeared beneath the surface, his young life snatched away by the cruel grip of fate. His legs got entangled in tree branches deep in the river. I trembled when I saw his pale body being pulled from the murky water. He was my nephew.

For me, as a 12-year-old, witnessing this tragedy was more than just a loss; it was a profound encounter with the silence of God. Amid chaos and desperation, my heart cried out in prayer, pleading for a miracle that never came. In the aftermath, questions flooded my mind: "God, are You there? Don't You care? Where are You? Are You real?" At that time, He was the silent God.

I believe that in moments of profound grief and confusion, it's natural to question the very existence of God and wrestle with doubts that threaten to engulf us. Yet, as I would later discover, it's the asking of these questions that helped me draw closer to the heart of God.

The Scriptures remind us time and again of God's invitation to seek Him, to bring our doubts and fears before Him without reservation. In Matthew 7:7, Jesus Himself encourages us to ask, seek, and knock, assuring us that those who earnestly seek will find.

But asking questions isn't just about seeking answers; it's about cultivating a deeper relationship with the One who holds the answers. It's about laying bare our hearts before God, trusting Him with our deepest doubts and insecurities. As I would reflect in later years, perhaps our questions serve as a means of connecting with the wisdom of God that surpasses human understanding. Perhaps they lead us to intimacy with Him as we gain more faith and understanding.

In 1 Corinthians 1:24, we're reminded that Jesus is the wisdom of God incarnate, the embodiment of divine truth and understanding. And so, as we wrestle with our questions, we are invited to journey deeper into the heart of God, allowing His wisdom to illuminate our minds and hearts.

So, to anyone who has ever questioned God in the face of tragedy or uncertainty, know that you are not alone. Your questions are not a sign of weakness or lack of faith; they are a testament to your honest desire to know God more deeply.

What if asking God questions is one way to cultivate a deeper relationship with Him? What if our questions become a door through which we could be vulnerable with Him? What if our questions open our minds to read the Scriptures with Spirit-empowered expectation instead of indifference and anger? If Jesus is the wisdom of God (1 Cor. 1:24), what if, by asking questions, we discover God; and by finding God, we find the answers?

Concluding Thought:

Our deepest questions and doubts often lead us to a more profound relationship with God. When we ask, He invites us into His heart of wisdom and love.

Closing Prayer:

Dear Lord, I come before You with all my questions and doubts. Help me to see that through these moments, You are drawing me closer to You. Grant me the wisdom and peace to trust Your answers, even when I do not understand. Lead me deeper into Your presence. In Jesus' name, Amen.

Reflection Questions:

1. Have you ever experienced a moment where you questioned God's presence or care? How did you respond?
2. How can you invite God into your questions and uncertainties?
3. What might God be trying to teach you through the questions you have about your life or faith?

Scripture for Meditation:

- Matthew 7:7 — "Ask, and it will be given to you; seek, and you will find; knock, and the door will be opened to you."
- 1 Corinthians 1:24 — "But to those whom God has called, both Jews and Greeks, Christ the power of God and the wisdom of God."
- Jeremiah 29:13 — "You will seek me and find me when you seek me with all your heart."

Week 51: The Joy Set Before Us

When we celebrate Christmas, we tend to focus on the joy of a newborn baby, the hope of new life, and the excitement of gifts. But one of the first gifts given to Jesus was myrrh—an embalming spice. It's a strange gift for a baby, isn't it? It reminds us of the bigger picture: Jesus was born to die, but not just any death—He came to die for us.

From the very beginning, Jesus' life had a purpose beyond what we could imagine. As soon as sin entered the world through Adam and Eve, humanity needed a Savior. Jesus came to fulfill that role, to take our place in death so that we could have life.

In Hebrews 12:2, we are told, *"For the joy set before Him, Jesus endured the cross, scorning its shame, and sat down at the right hand of the throne of God."* Jesus didn't shy away from His mission, even though it meant suffering and death. Why? Because He could see the joy beyond it—our salvation and eternal life with Him.

That's the joy of Christmas. Jesus didn't come just for the cradle—He came for the cross. And through His death and resurrection, He has brought us the greatest gift: eternal life.

As we celebrate this Christmas, let's remember that Jesus came to bring us hope, not just for today, but for eternity. He endured the cross because He saw the joy of our salvation, and now we can experience that same joy, knowing we are saved through Him.

Concluding Thought:

Christmas reminds us that Jesus came to give us life. The joy set before Him was our salvation, and that same joy is now ours. Let's embrace this season with gratitude for the greatest gift—eternal life through Christ.

Closing Prayer:

Lord, thank You for sending Jesus to be our Savior. Help me to see beyond the temporary and focus on the eternal joy that comes from knowing You. Thank You for the gift of salvation and the hope that Christmas brings. In Jesus' name, Amen.

Reflection Questions:

1. How does knowing Jesus came to die for you impact your view of Christmas?
2. How can you find joy in the struggles of life, knowing the joy that was set before Jesus?

Scripture for Meditation:

- **Hebrews 12:2 (NIV)** – "For the joy set before Him, He endured the cross, scorning its shame, and sat down at the right hand of the throne of God."
- **2 Timothy 1:9-10 (NIV)** – "He has saved us and called us to a holy life—not because of anything we have done but because of His own purpose and grace."

Week 52: Babysitting My Granddaughter

Three-month-old Zoe was especially bubbly this afternoon. She giggled and made sounds as if she wanted to talk. And there I was, dancing, singing baby songs, and speaking in baby talk myself. I felt a sense of joy wash over me.

Yet, as I reflected on the moment, I couldn't help but acknowledge how different this new chapter of my life truly is. Here I was, tending to a tiny human being who didn't really care about my previous education, experiences, or training. She didn't give a second thought to the leadership workshops, church planting sessions, or speech classes I had attended. Yes, those were valuable. But to my 3-month-old granddaughter, all those things are meaningless.

Looking back on my four decades of work as a pastor, I often find myself defined by various roles, accomplishments, and experiences. If I'm honest, I took pride in my education, achievements, and the recognition I received from the world around me. Yet now, it dawned on me: what happens when the very things that once defined me suddenly fade into the background? What happens when I'm faced with a new role that demands me to shed my former identities and embrace something entirely different? Can I still be me without those?

Such is the journey of transition that many of us may encounter. I find myself asking a fundamental question: "Who am I?" "Am I my education?" "Am I my experiences?" "My training?"

As I reflect on this question, the example set forth by our Lord Jesus Christ comes to mind. In His earthly ministry, Jesus did not seek recognition or praise for His divine nature or authority. Instead, He humbled Himself, taking on the form of a servant, and demonstrated the true essence of love through acts of service and compassion.

I believe that similarly, in our own lives, we are called to transcend the boundaries of our self-defined identities and embrace the call to serve others selflessly. Whether in the spotlight of recognition or in the quiet moments of anonymity, our true worth lies not in the titles we hold or the accolades we receive, but in our willingness to love and serve others with genuine humility.

My experience of transitioning from a world that praises personal achievements to one that demands selfless care for a helpless baby mirrors this profound truth. In caring for this child, I am reminded that my identity and significance are not found in what the world values.

I find comfort in the knowledge that my worth is not defined by my past accomplishments. Rather, it is found in my willingness to let Jesus live His life in me. And so, I find each moment with my three-month-old granddaughter very satisfying and fulfilling because it is not my diplomas, degree, or training that matters. It is the love of Christ that lies deep in my heart. I thank God for giving me this opportunity to share life with my granddaughter.

Concluding Thought:

Our true identity and worth are not found in our accomplishments or past roles, but in our ability to reflect Christ's love and humility. As we enter new seasons of life, may we embrace the call to serve others selflessly, finding joy in the simplicity of love and compassion.

Closing Prayer:

Heavenly Father, thank You for reminding us that our worth is not tied to our achievements or past roles, but in our relationship with You and our willingness to love and serve others. Help us to embrace new seasons of life with humility and joy, trusting that You will use us to reflect Your love, no matter the circumstances. In Jesus' name, we pray. Amen.

Reflection Questions:

1. How do you define your worth? Is it based on your accomplishments or on your relationship with God?
2. What are some areas of your life where you can serve others with humility, just as Christ served?
3. How can you embrace new roles and transitions in life while maintaining your identity in Christ?

Scripture for Meditation:

- Philippians 2:5-7 — "In your relationships with one another, have the same mindset as Christ Jesus: Who, being in very nature God, did not consider equality with God something to be used to His own advantage; rather, He made Himself nothing by taking the very nature of a servant."
- 1 Peter 5:6 — "Humble yourselves, therefore, under God's mighty hand, that He may lift you up in due time."
- Colossians 3:23 — "Whatever you do, work at it with all your heart, as working for the Lord, not for human masters."

Closing Remarks

As we come to the end of this devotional journey, may we be reminded that life itself is a journey—one filled with challenges, joys, uncertainties, and blessings. In every step we take, whether on smooth paths or rocky roads, God walks with us. The Father who created us, the Son who redeemed us, and the Spirit who guides us are always present, surrounding us with love and grace.

There is no step too small or too difficult for Him to notice. Every moment, even the hidden or forgotten ones, is seen and cherished by God. He invites us to trust Him, to lean into His presence, and to remember that we are never alone. As you continue forward, may you find peace in knowing that God is with you in every step, offering hope, strength, and the promise of His unwavering companionship.

Let us walk boldly, knowing that wherever our path leads, we are held in His love, now and always.

About the Author

Bermie Dizon has dedicated over 40 years to ministry as a pastor with Grace Communion International, serving in both the Philippines and the United States. His journey began in the Philippines in 1984, where he worked as a Ministerial Intern in Quezon City and Bulacan, later pastoring congregations in San Fernando, Pampanga; Tarlac; Cabanatuan; Angeles City; and Olongapo City. In 1992, he moved to Mindanao, ministering to communities in Davao City, Tagum, Kidapawan, General Santos City, and Digos.

In 1996, Bermie transitioned to ministry in the United States, starting as an associate pastor in Pasadena, CA. He helped establish a new church, NewLife, while simultaneously pastoring the Los Angeles congregation until 2019. His final years of full-time ministry were dedicated to the Beaumont and Glendora congregations before he retired in January 2024.

Throughout his pastoral journey, Bermie has encountered the joys, challenges, and surprises that come with a life of faith. His deep love for Jesus Christ fuels his compassion and commitment, extending beyond his home church to believers from diverse backgrounds. Bermie's passion for writing devotionals springs from this same love, weaving personal stories and spiritual reflections that offer warmth and wisdom to anyone seeking a closer relationship with God.

Now in retirement, Bermie volunteers as an ESL teacher with the San Gabriel Valley Literacy Council, an outreach that brings him immense joy. He remains an active member of Grace Communion Glendora and continues to share sermons with neighboring churches. He also dedicated five years to serving the homeless community near the Duarte riverbed, providing meals, hygiene items, clothing, and other essentials. He is presently the Chairman of the Board of Directors of a non-profit organization, **UJCC (United For Jesus Christian Community, Inc.)**

Bermie is happily married to Carmelita, a home health nurse. Together, they have four children and their spouses — Ben and Cassie, Carmel and Mat, Abel and Gelli, and David and Holli — as well as five beloved grandchildren: Mia, Urijah, Eli, Theo, and Zoe. Family is at the heart of Bermie's life. He cherishes every moment spent with. his grandchildren, whether visiting them or welcoming them home.

God, in Every Step

In his spare time, Bermie enjoys biking with friends and exploring Southern California's scenic trails, sometimes with his wife by his side. He's also an enthusiastic home cook, delighting in preparing dishes from around the world.

Through this devotional book, Bermie invites you to join him on a journey of faith, sharing in his love for Jesus and discovering God's presence in every step of life's path.

GOD,
IN EVERY STEP

God, in Every Step is a heartfelt collection of devotionals that invites readers to see God's hand in the ordinary moments of life. Pastor Bermie Dizon shares personal stories and reflections that span different life stages, from childhood to parenthood and struggles to triumphs. With relatable anecdotes and scriptural insights, each devotional points to the faithfulness and presence of God in every step we take, whether on a smooth path or through rocky terrain. It's a journey that reveals how God's grace can transform even the smallest, seemingly mundane experiences into divine encounters.

BERMIE DIZON

The book offers a comforting and honest look at the realities of faith, addressing topics like trust, surrender, waiting on God, and caring for others, especially those who are vulnerable or overlooked. Written with warmth and humility, God, In Every Step is a gentle reminder that God's love and guidance are constant companions, walking alongside us through every joy, trial, and unexpected turn. This collection is an invitation to pause, reflect, and recognize that in every moment—whether in the blessings or the mess—God is always near.

Made in the USA
Middletown, DE
04 February 2025